The GREAT REVEAL

THE SECRETS TO 'UNVEILING THE VEILED' FOR SUCH A TIME AS THIS!

DR. Y. BUR

Available Titles

ASITPLEASESGOD.COM

The Great Reveal

The Secrets to *'Unveiling the Veiled'* for Such a Time as This!

Copyright © 2020 by Dr. Y. Bur. All rights reserved.

Visit www.RoarPublishingGroup.com for more information. No part of this publication may be reproduced, stored in a retrieval system, or transmitted in any way, electronic, mechanical, photocopy, recording, or otherwise, without the author's prior permission except as provided by USA copyright law.

Book design copyright © 2020 by R.O.A.R. International Group. All rights reserved.

R.O.A.R. Publishing Group
581 N. Park Ave. Ste. #725
Apopka, FL 32704
www.RoarPublishingGroup.com
Dr.YBur@gmail.com

Published in the United States of America
ISBN: 978-1-948936-48-4
$22.88

www.RoarPublishingGroup.com

ASITPLEASESGOD.COM

Table of Contents

INTRODUCTION 7

CHAPTER 1 13
   KINGDOM TRANSPARENCY 13

CHAPTER 2 25
   HEAVENLY LINGUISTICS 25

CHAPTER 3 39
   SPIRITUAL INSIGHT 39

CHAPTER 4 49
   FIX YOUR CROWN 49

CHAPTER 5 59
   SPIRITUAL LAMPSTAND 59

CHAPTER 6 73
   THRONE ROOM 73

CHAPTER 7 89
   HEAVENLY OF HEAVENS 89

CHAPTER 8 107
   THE GREAT REVEAL 107

CHAPTER 9 125
   BULLIES UNVEILED 125

CHAPTER 10 143

SILENT WHISPERS	143
CHAPTER 11	**155**
THE SPIRITUAL SENSATION	155
CHAPTER 12	**169**
UNVEILING THE VEILED	169

Introduction

When we are Spiritually Ill-Equipped to handle life or its issues, we will seek comfort from something or someone to avoid openly breaking down or secretly melting away. It is for this reason that many of us fall by the wayside or outright make ungodly choices, reaping coals upon our heads, regardless of whether we admit it or not. However, all is not lost, especially if we take the time to recognize it, own our truth, repent, learn the lessons, make the appropriate changes, and share the wisdom we have learned to build and inspire ourselves and others, As It Pleases God.

My goal is to provide the Spiritual Tools for *The Great Reveal* and bring our Spiritual Awareness to the forefront, As It Pleases God. Doing so ensures that we can recognize our differences or inconsistencies while making the appropriate corrections needed to enter the Kingdom of Heaven with clean hands and a pure heart.

We cannot think for a minute that we do not have a role to play in the Kingdom of God, nor can we think that we do not have to prepare for it as well. Why must we prepare? Our Spiritual Training Ground and *The Great Reveal* are comprised of how we handle our everyday living, thinking, being, growing, and becoming.

What is the purpose of being able to handle whatever with whomever? If we cannot deal with the Vicissitudes and Seasons of life, we will crumble, fold, or bow down under pressure, making us unfit for Kingdom Use, *As It Pleases God*. Clearly, we do not need to be perfect; still, we must govern ourselves accordingly. Listed below are a few examples of our accordingly in the Eye of God, but not limited to such:

- ☐ If we cannot handle the issues of life, we will become unable to solve real problems or think on our feet, causing a Spiritual Disconnect.

- ☐ If we cannot control our tongues, we will speak out of turn, causing our loose lips to sink ships or traumatize others.

- ☐ If we cannot perfect our perception, we will misinterpret what is being said in or out of the Kingdom, thwarting our Spiritual Receptors.

- ☐ If we cannot control our emotions, we will become easily offended, allowing the psyche to take over to feed the Spiritual Warring from within.

- ☐ If we cannot control our lying tongue, we will lie at the drop of a dime without a conscience or self-correction.

- ☐ If we cannot control our feelings of hate, we will become debaucherous, biased, and rotten in the Eye of God.

- ☐ If we cannot love, we will exhibit unlovable or corruptible behaviors toward others while appearing right in our own eyes. Then again, we will be unable to exhibit the Fruits of the Spirit or behave Christlike, *As It Pleases God*.

- ☐ If we cannot become peaceful, we will become combative, disobedient, dull, or disruptive in or out of the Kingdom of God.

- ☐ If we cannot listen, we will develop a deaf ear to God, ourselves, others, and most of all, our Predestined Blueprint.

- ☐ If we cannot be kind, we will become an unkind or unruly individual filled with jealousy, envy, pride, greed, coveting, and competitiveness while appearing right.

- ☐ If we cannot forgive, we will become intolerable, cruel, hateful, or abrasive while pretending to be the victim.

- ☐ If we cannot become teachable, we will miss the Divine Message of the Kingdom, forcing us into a cycle of déjà vu.

Above all, God requires us to become Spiritually Consistent with a work-in-progress mentality and tone. What do mentality and tone have to do with *The Great Reveal* in the Eye of God? He requires us to operate with Christlike Character outside of the four walls of the Church. Why is this a requirement for Believers? It is due to innocent people getting hurt or traumatized by our ungodliness while we pretend to be Godly, Holy, or Heaven-Sent.

As a forewarning, if someone cannot be transparent, we must exercise extreme caution. What is the reason for such caution? We all have issues hidden under different labels, even if we pretend to be perfect, polished, or pristine. Pointing the finger of judgment without opening our hands to help is a sign of self-righteousness, lack of humility, or outright selfishness that will lead to more significant issues down the line.

Why would we have more issues than solutions? Self-righteousness, the lack of humility, or outright selfishness contain masks of deception, and this is what the enemy uses to gain entry into the Mind, Body, and Soul to sift us or turn us against ourselves.

According to the Heavenly of Heavens, as long as we have breath in our bodies, we are all a work-in-progress and must Spiritually Till our own grounds, working on ourselves continuously for the Greater Good. Why must we become a work-in-progress as Believers? We all have room for growth because our Mind, Body, Soul, and Spirit must be fed. What does this mean? We can choose what we feed ourselves and decline what we do not want. Then again, we can allow someone to do it for us or allow life to do it.

From my perspective, I would not play Russian roulette with my Mind, Body, Soul, or Spirit under any circumstances. Why not? I do not want to be tossed to and fro by the issues of life. Nor do I want to be placed into a cycle of déjà vu, redoing what I can get right the first time around.

The truth of the matter is that if we have a desire to understand the psyche of man, we must redirect our teachings back to the Bible, *As It Pleases God*. Can we achieve healing outside of the Bible? Absolutely. Then, why do we need the Bible? Healing outside of Spiritual means will only give us limited access, time, knowledge, courage, how-to, and power. All of which are designed to lead us back to SPIRITUALITY in Earthen Vessel.

Why are we limited outside of Spirituality? First, we are Spiritual Beings having a human experience. Secondly, if we do not get to the root cause of our issues, it creates other underlying, topical, or superficial issues. All of our attempts, patches, or fixes are only temporary, causing us to revisit our issues continually or outright provide phoniness, masks, justifications, or cover-ups.

For example, the best analogy I can provide is similar to having an open sore and placing a Band-Aid on our issues or developing a scab over our traumas to prevent their reopening. Yet, once the sore is bumped, triggered, or reopened by something or someone, it will remind us of the sting of pain, causing us to react or deflate while having to go through the same process of temporary healing all over again.

According to the Kingdom of Heaven, modern-day or old-school perspectives do not change God; He is consistent regardless of what we think or believe. Therefore, we must step outside of ourselves to gather the necessary information to understand the Mind of God, as well as the INDIVIDUALIZED MESSAGES He has for each of us. Once accomplished, we will have a better understanding of ourselves and others without thwarting our Mission or that of another.

Why would we thwart our Divine Mission? Self-sabotage is real. Without self-understanding, we cannot truly understand the

Secret Elements of the Spirit due to our Spiritual Unreadiness; therefore, we will remain veiled until we are ready.

Now, regardless of our level of unreadiness, it does not mean God will not use us as a Vessel; He will use anything or anyone to accomplish His Mission. But more importantly, when it comes down to Spiritual Elevation, we must become trained in this area through viable Levels of Spirituality.

Why must we have Spiritual Training, *As It Pleases God*? It is God's way of saving us from ourselves or preventing the misuse of Spiritual Authority or Power. What does this mean? We need to become properly equipped to avoid Spiritual Oppression, Correction, Obliteration, or Generational Curses.

The moment we can take Spiritual Principles and apply them in our walk of life, we will find our walk with God becoming easier, understandable, and pliable. How do we genuinely understand Spiritual Principles? We must learn how to read the Bible for ourselves to receive our personalized messages. There is no need to become a Bible Scholar; all we need is to become a Willing and Trustworthy Scholar, *As It Pleases God*. Why do we not have a Universal Message? God's messages may vary from person to person. Plus, He does not pride Himself on using cookie-cutter methods of operation to prevent us, as humans, from breaking the Spiritual Codes of Spirituality and our DNA. If we do not develop our Spiritual Insight, *As It Pleases Him*, we can fall prey to misinterpreting or misreading the message. Therefore, we must get all of our Spiritual Faculties or Tools up and running to ensure we do not miss the mark or pray amiss.

For starters, if we begin applying the Fruits of the Spirit to our lives, thoughts, behaviors, attitudes, and demeanor, we gain the upper hand in gleaning from the Holy Spirit. What does this mean? We put ourselves in the Spiritual Category to have a *Spirit to Spirit* encounter, a Spiritual Ushering, or a Divine Download of Kingdom Principles.

The Spiritual Lantern of God requires us to take a journey into self, getting rid of all the gritty, mud-slinging sludge that has the potential to tarnish the Image of God, bringing shame to our name and His. What is the reason for doing so? If we do not take the time to purify ourselves, we could unawaringly get sludge on the innocent.

Just keep in mind that we will all have strengths and weaknesses...the goal is to become aware of them without burying or hiding our truth. Why do we need to know this information? If we do not know it, the enemy will pounce on us in the areas of our hidden weaknesses to crush our self-esteem, creating a bed of self-doubt, insecurity, or an identity crisis. Whereas if we own our truth, it decreases the feelings of humiliation or running from one thing to the next. Plus, we become open to accepting help from another to become better without becoming bitter, jealous, envious, covetous, prideful, or self-destructive.

God knows our limitations and weaknesses, and He wants us to know them as well. Why must we know about them? It helps us search for the Spiritual Tools He has already provided to assist us, but we must become grateful to open ourselves up to *The Great Reveal*.

What is the need for gratefulness? From experience, most often, our Blessings or Birthrights are hidden in our handicaps, traumas, or weaknesses. If we overlook them without working on them or working at them, we can miss the mark. So, I would advise that we take nothing for granted, regardless of how it may appear to the naked eye.

According to the Heavenly of Heavens, God has given everyone at least one Gift or Talent for their Divine Purpose. Yet, it must be sought after if we do not know what it is. How is it possible to seek what we do not know or understand? Most often, outside of our weaknesses, handicaps, and traumas, our Divine Purpose can also lie in the area of our Passion, Creativity, or both. Although everyone is different, we must engage in our own journey for ourselves, Spiritually Tilling our own ground.

No one can pursue your inner-born Destiny better than you. Really? Yes, really! The Predestined Blueprint is already written on the tablet of your heart; it only needs UNVEILING, *As It Pleases God*. So, if one desires to partake in the *Unveiling Process*, let us go a little deeper into *The Great Reveal*. I promise not to disappoint.

Chapter 1

KINGDOM TRANSPARENCY

According to the Heavenly of Heavens, as Spiritual Beings, we were designed to be relational, provoking the element of thought through our words, actions, reactions, demeanor, and problem-solving capabilities. Unfortunately, to our detriment, if we digress with this DNA-tical formality, it creates a formal breakdown of the human psyche and our *Kingdom Transparency.*

In living our best lives, regardless of our intents or lack of understanding of our Divine Expectations, causing known or unknown inactiveness or reactiveness as opposed to positive proactiveness, *As It Pleases God*, creates Spiritual Taboos. Blasphemy, right? Absolutely not! Here is what we must know: *"My people are destroyed for lack of knowledge. Because you have rejected knowledge, I also will reject you from being priest for Me; Because you have forgotten the law of your God, I also will forget your children."* Hosea 4:6.

The Cycle of Knowledge is never-ending, even if we decline the Divine Call or Mandate. We are taught to become the Teacher, positively or negatively. So, we must become cautious about what we are teaching, regardless of our condition, status, intellect, etc. What is the purpose of doing so? Whatever we set in motion becomes the fruit of tomorrow, the next day, and so on, until the cycle is broken, enhanced, or stolen. Once again, this works both positively and negatively, but we always want to stay on the spectrum's positive side to ensure our fruits remain in the Kingdom, *As It Pleases God*.

The goal is to condition the mind to have good, Godly, and fruitful thoughts playing in the background continuously. Why must we engage in positive mental playback? To ward off the negativity of what is happening around us that would cause our minds to jump the track, or to prevent us from becoming extremely sensitive to feedback.

How is it possible for the mind to jump the track? We all have positive, negative, and lustful triggers; therefore, we must know what to engage in and what to avoid. For example, suppose we take one step at a time to interject positivity when negativity presents itself, use Biblical Affirmations, exhibit the Fruits of the Spirit, and focus on the Promises and Blessings of God. In this case, we can ward off the negative mind germs designed to make us sick from the inside out. Does this work? Absolutely. Regardless of what we do, say, or become, our minds will think continuously, positively or negatively. So, we may as well make it think for us and not against us.

In mastering *Kingdom Transparency*, we must become familiar with painting mental pictures, *As It Pleases God*. Why are positive mental pictures beneficial for Believers? If we paint mental pictures to please ourselves, we will tend to get the Divine Message wrong more than we get it right, especially when dealing with paid clicks, becoming an influencer, or branding ourselves to be the ones with the answers. Here is the deal: The mind can create anything it wants and justify itself as being correct with an element of truth, but NOT THE EXACT TRUTH. And, when dealing with the Heavenly of Heavens, when a Spiritual Decree is made, we cannot get it wrong, especially when laying it on the doorstep of the Holy Spirit or spreading rotten, debauched fruits without love, mercy, and compassion.

So, suppose we do not train our minds from God's Divine Perspective, including Him in all things. In this case, we will become easily brainwashed, manipulated, hotwired, or cast ill-willed divinations in the Name of God, especially when He did not give the Decree. How do I know? The Holy Spirit has Spiritual Principles that must be followed, and if we do not know what they are or if we are not operating in them, it is NOT the Holy Spirit operating. Really? Yes, really! For this reason, pretense has become our Spiritual Kryptonite.

The Holy Spirit has a Vibrational VOICE, painting a relevant picture for the ones being spoken to without having to call a person's name publicly! For the record, if a Prophet of the Most High God has to call a person out publicly without meeting the person privately...The Spiritual Decree is Spiritually NULL and VOID.

Why is the exposure Spiritually NULL and VOID, especially when it is accurate? Once again, Spiritual Protocol was not followed, *As It Pleases God*, and the broadcasting in a public setting can be reversed back to that individual. Really? Yes, really! Unfortunately, this is one of the reasons we have Believers fighting against themselves behind closed doors and outing each other for clicks, likes, followers, or a dollar.

God is looking for our heart postures, mindsets, fruits, and character traits to align with Him, or the misalignment therein. Is there really a Spiritual Protocol when dealing with *Kingdom Transparency*? Absolutely. Here are the steps, but not limited to such:

- ☐ *"If your brother sins against you, go and tell him his fault between you and him alone. If he hears you, you have gained your brother."* Matthew 18:15.

- ☐ *"But if he will not hear, take with you one or two more, that 'by the mouth of two or three witnesses every word may be established.' "* Matthew 18:16.

- ☐ *"If he refuses to listen to them, tell it to the church; and if he refuses to listen even to the church, let him be to you as a Gentile and a tax collector."* Matthew 18:17.

How can a Spiritual Decree be reversed, particularly when exhibiting our First Amendment Rights? According to the Heavenly of Heavens, Spiritual Laws take precedence over any manmade laws, even if we think we are above the law or below it. For the record, God is Supreme! Now, to answer the question, when dealing with the faults of another, here is what we must know:

- ☐ *"Assuredly, I say to you, whatever you bind on earth will be bound in heaven, and whatever you loose on earth will be loosed in heaven."* Matthew 18:18.

- ☐ *"Again I say to you that if two of you agree on earth concerning anything that they ask, it will be done for them by My Father in heaven."* Matthew 18:19.

What does this mean? Simply put, we must be careful about what we set in motion with our mouths, especially when it has nothing to do with us. Releasing selfish or ill-willed negativity brings negativity, period! More importantly, if we release negativity into the Heavenly of Heavens, it will be rejected and marked returned to sender! On the other hand, for the Heavens to bring positivity, we must release what is good and scripturally sound, *As It Pleases God*.

When dealing with *Kingdom Transparency*, it is always best to build up another without tearing them down. Why are we required to build, especially when people are making their best attempts to break us down to the core? We do not know what God is using to Spiritually Train, Prepare, Appoint, Teach, or Chastise. For this reason, the Bible says, *"Touch not My anointed ones, and do My prophets no harm."* Psalm 105:15. If we come between God and His Divine Will, we can absorb the judgment of the ones we are judging. How so? We will have that same behavior appear in someone we love, especially in our children.

If we master our Mental Designs, *As It Pleases God*, and with the Fruits of the Spirit, we will cease to have issues with blockages of self-expression, self-mirroring, and self-control. How does this process help us? It opens the mind to think, process, and articulate on a different level...A Kingdom Level, to be exact.

When adding the Holy Trinity into our equational efforts, it causes us to think before speaking, judging, or assuming. The value of having individualized thoughts, emotions, or languages that cannot be duplicated or emulated is the ideal Spiritual Grounding needed for *Kingdom Transparency*. Is this not a contradiction? In the Eye of God, we must master properly seasoning what to say, when, how, why, and with whom. Please allow me to Spiritually Align: *"Let your speech always be with grace, seasoned with salt, that you may know how you ought to answer each one."* Colossians 4:6.

How do we make *Kingdom Transparency* make sense? It is about being honest and open about our journey, struggles, mishaps, and growth. Unless our secret qualms are verbally spoken, it remains speculation, and then again, some things need to remain in our prayer closet.

More importantly, our Spiritual Transparency is with God first, ourselves, and then others. Putting people, places, and things into their proper perspective, *As It Pleases God*, involves a willingness to share personal experiences, doubts, and questions with others in order to foster deeper connections, encouragement, and testimonial support. Why is it essential in the Eye of God? For healing. Is this Biblical? I would have it no other way. *"Confess your trespasses to one another, and pray for one another, that you may be healed."* James 5:16.

The scriptures tell us time and time again to keep a guard over our mouths, then how is it possible to guard our tongues when God requires transparency? Spiritual Transparency does not mean broadcasting our lives over the internet or in public. What it means is that we must repent, turning our tests, failures, or mishaps into a Testimony as a Formal Testament for those coming behind us. Here lies the dilemma: premature transparency will cause the enemy to use our weaknesses against us. How? If we take it to worldly means before taking it to God, we are already defying Spiritual Protocol.

For example, if we decide to stop smoking and then broadcast our deliverance to the world without cluing God in on the matter, it means we are self-sufficient from a worldly perspective. So, in this gloating phase of self-gratification, three days later, we go about our way to cast out the nicotine addiction from another person. Lo and behold, a week later, the individual who engages in the casting out, only transferred the Spirit back onto themselves. As a result, they have now gone from smoking one pack of cigarettes a day to smoking three. Why did this happen? From the beginning to the end, God was nowhere in the equation, which caused Spiritual Instability, giving the enemy leverage to reenter its host for not following Spiritual Protocol. This flawed transparency process only provides an open haven for failure, embarrassment, defeat, or blame. Playing God or becoming a demigod will cause the joke to fall on us without any form of Spiritual Staying Power.

Premature transparency without training, healing, or deliverance is dangerous to the Body of Christ. Why is this dangerous for untrained or unhealed Believers? If we are trying to deliver someone from the same Spiritual Vice that we are not delivered from or not adequately trained in casting out, the enemy will have a field day, tossing us to and fro in turmoil from the inside out.

Spiritual Battles are won with Spiritual Armor, and if we have not taken the time to suit up Spiritually, the enemy will hang us out to dry. Why would this happen, especially as Believers who are Holy Ghost-Filled and Fire-Baptized? He, meaning the enemy, knows our approach is unjustifiable and out of order; plus, he knows our hidden weaknesses. As a result, it gives him more momentum in the sifting process to our potential detriment. How is this possible without our permission? Somehow, we opted out of becoming a work-in-progress, *As It Pleases God,* and came into agreement with the enemy through our thoughts, words, actions, desires, or whatever.

Just so we are clear, one does not need to be a Spiritual Elite to cast down or cast out. They simply need to follow proper Spiritual Protocol, taking things to God first. Once done, then we can deal with ourselves while suiting up with Spiritual Armor to deal with others on a case-by-case basis.

What is the best way to approach Spiritual Transparency? It is imperative to deal with our transparency in this order, but not limited to such:

- ☐ We must own our issues, circumstances, or situations and come to terms with them, *As It Pleases God*.
- ☐ We must repent.
- ☐ We must take it to God in prayer, secretly.
- ☐ We must fast if necessary.
- ☐ We must understand our point of erring.
- ☐ We must pinpoint our 'Why' in the issue, circumstance, or situation.
- ☐ We must understand the effects from a Spiritual Perspective.
- ☐ We must know how it affected us from a worldly standpoint.
- ☐ We must find the scriptures or Biblical stories relating to our issues.
- ☐ We must streamline positive affirmations to circumvent rehashing or repeating the mishap.
- ☐ We must create a win-win or find the good, making it work in our favor.
- ☐ We must share the Testimony to encourage, build, and motivate from a Christlike Perspective, using the Fruits of the Spirit.

Even if we do not get all the answers or revelations at once, do not panic. The goal is to write whatever we get down. By having it in writing, we can revisit it as God fills in the blanks of what we did not get previously. Frankly, this is how He works with me, and He will do likewise with all who avail themselves to the process.

As a Body of Christ, we judge others with false truths based on our perception, resulting in Commutative Disorder in the Kingdom. When in all actuality, we should become examples of God's Grace and Mercy by showing, mentoring, teaching, and encouraging the WAY to the Kingdom instead. According to Kingdom Principles, God is not looking for us to minister to others from the pulpit; He expects us to reach ourselves and others by ministering through our daily journey. What does this mean? According to scripture, it says, *"Go into all the world and preach the gospel to every creature."* Mark 16:15. *"And they went out and preached everywhere, the Lord working with them and confirming the word through the accompanying signs."* Mark 16:20. Our daily walk should become a representative of Godliness by exhibiting the Fruits of the Spirit and Christlike Character, reflecting kindness, compassion, thoughtfulness, helpfulness, gratefulness, proactiveness, and mercy everywhere, not just somewhere!

We cannot live like a saint on one day a week or within the four walls of the church. Then, behave like a hellion on wheels for six days, dragging innocent people through the dirt or refusing to pull them out of the mud to avoid getting our hands dirty. If we proclaim to be Christlike and cannot pull our brothers and sisters out of the mud when it is in our power to do so, we have a little more Spiritual Training to do in Christlike Protocols. Spiritually, when we know better and willfully choose not to do better, this is a recipe for disaster from the inside out. Always remember, we can run, but we cannot hide from our truth!

If we desire to become one of the Spiritual Elites for the Kingdom of Heaven, we must develop our Spiritual Language. Is there another way around this? Yes. We can stay where we are, digressing in our Spiritual Formality, doing our own thing. We can also move forward without God, being led by worldliness, bound by our lusts and materialism. Or, we can outright go to the dark side, gaining superficial strength. They all work temporarily, still leaving an inner void of the more, more, more, or the gimme, gimme, gimme attitude. Ungratefulness and avoiding God always do the trick on the human psyche, particularly when we do not develop our Spiritual Language as we should.

Regardless of how God is portrayed, there are certain things that He requires of us if we desire to become one of the Elites in the Spiritual Realm. What does He require? First and foremost, He requires growth. Secondly, He requires us to understand. Thirdly, He requires us to mature. And fourthly, He requires us to share. Now, to perfect the art of doing so, we need to do a few things:

- ☐ We must have respect for God, ourselves, and others, including everything He created.
- ☐ We need to think for ourselves in words, images, and actions.
- ☐ We need to learn when to lead and when to follow.
- ☐ We need to turn negatives into positives at the drop of a dime.
- ☐ We must look for the good, positive, productive, and fruitful in all things.
- ☐ We must perfect the art of listening and understanding.
- ☐ We must become savvy in the way we speak, choosing our words carefully and kindly.
- ☐ We must read, period. There is no exception to this rule.
- ☐ We must fine-tune our instincts, conscience, and senses, *As It Pleases God*.
- ☐ We must safeguard our integrity, using it often without willfully violating or traumatizing others.
- ☐ We must develop Christlike Character using the Fruits of the Spirit (Love, Joy, Peace, Patience, Kindness, Goodness, Faithfulness, Gentleness, and Self-Control).
- ☐ We must document, document, document.

We must write down or keep track of instructions, concepts, precepts, ideas, thoughts, etc. Once again, there is no exception to this rule. According to the Heavenly of Heaven, '*I got it*' is not going to get it, especially if it is not documented properly. Spiritually, it leaves too much room for the enemy to steal our Seeds of Thought, Wisdom, Instructions, etc.

But more importantly, we are commanded to write. According to scripture, if one has a desire to become one of the Spiritual Elites, it says, *"Write the things which you have seen, and the things which are, and the things which will take place after this."* Revelation 1:19.

From the Beginning in the Garden of Eden, if we study God and His method of operation, we will understand that He has zero tolerance for shady, cunning, and deceptive character traits. Even if we feel as if we are getting away with things on the surface, we will still feel the tug or the sting from within. However, we may cover it up, but this is okay. Why is this okay in the Eye of God? In the same way, we cover whatever it is up, we can uncover it as well. We are never too deep where God cannot draw us out.

In changing our narrative to a Kingdom Building one, we need to become willing, able, and ready to adhere to His Will and Ways, *As It Pleases Him*. In *Kingdom Transparency*, God frowns upon those who double-dip where He has already dapped! What does this mean? The double-dip is when we straddle the fence between worldliness and Spirituality, and we only come to God to beg for THINGS or when we are in trouble. The dap is the Revelatory Seal that God has placed upon our life and His Word. Is this Biblical? Of course, *"No one can serve two masters; for either he will hate the one and love the other, or else he will be loyal to the one and despise the other. You cannot serve God and mammon."* Matthew 6:24.

Most often, double-dipping is found in those who secretly pimp God and His Word for selfish gain. Do we not have the free will to do whatever, whenever, and however? Yes, we do have free will, but it does not give us the right to negligently use the Word of God as our pawn when it has already been Spiritually Sealed.

Once again, God has already SEALED the beginning to the end of time in His Word, especially in the Book of Revelation. But more importantly, Job 33:14-16 gives us a few details about seals; it says, *"For God may speak in one way, or in another, yet man does not perceive it. In a dream, in a vision of the night, when deep sleep falls upon men, while slumbering on their beds, then He opens the ears of men, and seals their instruction."* The moment we think we do not have what it takes to embark upon this Spiritual Journey, just keep in mind, *"He seals the hand of every man, that all men may know His work."* Job 37:7. So, we cannot play dirty!

As life would have it, if we choose to continue to play dirty to get what we want, we will find our worldly veil will develop a colorless, odorless, and tasteless krypton. With or without our permission, in due time, this type of krypton debilitates us or anyone who enters our environment from the inside out with Spiritual Blindness, Deafness, and Muteness. Is this Biblical? In scripture, this is often referred to as the Pit; it says, *"Then he looks at men and says, 'I have sinned, and perverted what was right, and it did not profit me.' He will redeem his soul from going down to the Pit, and his life shall see the light. Behold, God works all these things, twice, in fact, three times with a man, to bring back his soul from the Pit, that he may be enlightened with the light of life."* Job 33:27-30. We all have the power and authority to ask, seek, knock, or find by tapping into the *Heavenly Linguistics* with clean hands and a pure heart, *As It Pleases God.*

Chapter 2

HEAVENLY LINGUISTICS

The Linguistic Relativity of Spirituality has us competing against each other, trying to determine who is right or wrong. When, in fact, no one is 100% right or 100% wrong, making the Mysteries of God Heavenly and unawaringly sought after by all. According to our DNA-tical Design, we need God, who is the Creator of it all. We did not create ourselves, and without Him, there is no us! When it is all said and done, once it comes down to our *Heavenly Linguistics*, the Holy Spirit and the Blood of Jesus are here to correct the correctable, anoint the anointable, lead the leadable, govern the governable, help the helpless, illuminate darkness, speak to the listener, provide messages to the messenger, give wisdom to the wise, bring life to the dead, unyoke the yoked, and break the chains of those in bondage.

When we prioritize God in all things, we can become guided by the Holy Spirit through the Blood of Jesus. Why is this so important? God has created Spiritual Systems, Concepts, Laws, and Precepts to work on our behalf. If we interject our systems to override His, we will have issues at some point in our equational living.

Taking God out of the equation of anything places us in a self-reliant position, causing us to trip up when we should be standing tall or standing tall when we need to exhibit humility. In my opinion, this particular mindset will cause us to rub God and others the wrong way. How? Pompousness is a surefire way to invoke secret envy, jealousy, coveting, pride, and debauchery in those who despise us, wish ill will, or seek our demise.

Our verbal or non-verbal language says a lot about who we are without us having to say one word. Why is our language so important? Contrary to what most would think, listed below are a few things we should take note of when it comes down to our Spiritual Language:

- ☐ What we see affects our language.
- ☐ What we hear affects our language.
- ☐ What comes out of our mouths affects our language.
- ☐ What we think affects our language.
- ☐ Our perception affects our language.
- ☐ Our biases or culture affect our language.
- ☐ Our hidden or open traumas affect our language.
- ☐ Our denial affects our language.
- ☐ Our truth affects our language.
- ☐ Our Gifts, Calling, Creativity, or Talents affect our language.
- ☐ Our Spirituality affects our language.
- ☐ Our Divine Destiny or Blueprint affects our language.

Our experiences in life are wrapped in the perceptional language of our reality, spreading outwardly. What does this mean? How we view our lives from the inside out determines our outcome, positively or negatively. Our Mind, Body, Soul, and Spirit speak to communicate interactively, causing the Vessel of God to work in unison. If one breaks the communication chain, it is reflected in how we feel, think, behave, and what we say. So, from my perspective, we must pay close attention to our vicissitudinous signals. The Vicissitudes of Life are real, and if we do not pay attention, we can become sideswiped, stepped on or over, yoked, or soul-tied, period.

With the ever-changing life we live, the Vicissitudes of our Spiritual Language are designed to invoke a relational comfort within those we come in contact with. What does this mean? We can speak their language in a Godly manner to naturally penetrate their core without jumping through hoops. How is this possible? It is through the Holy Spirit. Once we genuinely connect to the Holy Trinity (The Father, Son, and Holy Spirit) as a Spiritual Vessel, it is His responsibility to clue us in on what to say, when to say it, where to say it, how to say it, why to say it, and, more importantly, the unction to plead the 5th.

On the other hand, if we are vexing people or we have to play psychological mind games, it is imperative that we step back into the Spiritual Classroom. Why must we head back into the student's posture as Believers? Our Spiritual Language has become worldly, especially when our words cut wounds into the heart of man instead of healing them. Our Christlike Character should set an example for others to do likewise, but this should be a red flag for us if someone avoids mirroring our behavior.

The value we are seeking is ready to avail itself to us, but there is a catch! For our *Heavenly Linguistics*, we need Spiritual Insight from God Himself. Our soul is very fickle, and if we do not take the time to understand, nurture, and correct it, we will find it becoming resistant and selfish by nature, causing secret or open Spiritual Anguish and Blindness. What does this mean? We will begin to fight against ourselves with our thought patterns, perceptions, and biases, drawing more toward the negative and dark side of life for comfort. How can we alter this effect? It can be warded off by applying Biblical Principles into our daily lives and using the Fruits of the Spirit.

Little do we know, God's more in-depth responses are wrapped in our questions, and if we do not master this Art of the Kingdom, we will have a lot of unanswered questions, dreams, prayers, or whatever. For the most part, no one likes walking around and not being *In The Know*, even if we pretend we do not care. But when it comes down to the Elements of the Spirit, God will not hang us out to dry without allowing us to change for the better to give or inspire the Greater Hope from within.

The Questionables of God have a profound impact on our Divine Spirituality, especially if we dare to master our perception, as well as our responses to His Blessings and Correction. To say the least, our reflections of Him will clear our Spiritual Vision to the 10th Degree when we can ask the right questions without asking amiss. Moreover, when we respond with the correct answers, reactions, and actions pleasing to His Will and Ways when He questions us, it helps us Spiritually Align, *As It Pleases Him*. God is very precise, and He requires us to become this way as well.

How can we become Spiritually Precise? The grassroots of our faith in Spiritual Propellation begins with asking God, ourselves, and others the right fact-finding questions. Although we are all different, we can learn how to break any form of barrier by asking:

- ☐ What?
- ☐ When?
- ☐ Where?
- ☐ How?
- ☐ Why?
- ☐ With Whom?

Why do we need to ask questions and receive answers? Frankly, if we do not avail ourselves to the Questionables of life, we become led by our assumptions, conditioning, biases, and the list goes on. For this reason, from a Spiritual Perspective, when asking questions and documenting answers, we must be true to ourselves, and we must also master our ability to listen to the Voice of God, *As It Pleases Him*.

How do we recognize the Voice of God? It varies from person to person, situation to situation, relationship to relationship, and so on. Nonetheless, we are able to communicate *Spirit to Spirit*. Our Inner Spirit-Man can recognize His Voice if we AWAKEN it. How do we go about doing so? We must *Ask* for its presence by calling it forth, *Seeking* the ways and things of God, and *finding* our truth from within or our Gifts, Talents, or Calling. But more importantly, we must consciously and attentively listen for His still, small VOICE from within.

What if we cannot hear His Voice? We must keep trying. Just because we do not hear anything one day does not mean we will not hear from Him the next. God has a way of teaching or developing us through silence; besides, it also creates patience within an anxious soul as well. Keep in mind that we operate on His terms, *As It Pleases Him*, not on ours to please ourselves or our ego.

Here is the deal: our Spiritual Flow operates in peace; however, if we are all over the place Mentally, Physically, Emotionally, and Spiritually, we will become Spiritually Blocked even if we pretend to have it all together. Why does this happen? To receive Spiritual Transfers from God, our Heavenly Father, we cannot create roadblocks or barriers inhibiting the *Spirit to Spirit* communication process.

Our Spiritual Wires can become crossed, inhibiting our ability to receive the correct messages from God due to some form of Spiritual Blindness, Deafness, or Muteness. Listen, when we receive mixed or wrong messages, it will cause the inner chatter to overshadow our righteousness or Christlike Character. Over time, if left uncorrected, it will cause us to justify and rationalize negativity, unjust behavior, ungodly character traits, or outright selfishness. Why does this happen? Our Spiritual Dialogue has become so commercialized with superficial images of the Blessings and Promises of God that we begin making up stuff to appease ourselves.

Worldly materialism, appearing real from a Spiritual Perspective, will cause us to miss the mark with God as we pray amiss. Just so we are clear, before we move on, the Blessings and Promises of God are often wrapped in the people, places, and things money cannot buy. In addition, it is also hidden in a problem, or it is intertwined with something or someone we would reject due to our hidden biases. For this reason, we must continuously do a check-up from the neck up to avoid overlooking what is designed to bless us, and we must also listen to what our lives are saying to and about us. Why do we need to go through this process? The worldly hoopla about God's Method-of-Operation will cause us to become yoked, soul-tied, or sifted to the point where we will not realize we have gone astray while appearing right in our own eyes.

God's Dialogue is not an outer experience as most would think; it is an inner experience! Therefore, we must come to ourselves and look within, developing our inner Spiritual Voice. How do we know if we are on the right track? The moment we make a positive impact with our unspoken words through our actions, attitudes, and behaviors through the silent use of the Fruits of the Spirit, we are well on our way. Unfortunately, this is not an overnight process. According to the Heavenly of Heavens, we must put in the work to develop ourselves from the inside out to ensure we are Spiritually Synchronized, our motives are pure, and our perception is positively set to what God has in mind, *As It Pleases Him.*

Our *Heavenly Linguistics,* or The Blueprint of God, is already written on the tablet of our hearts; we simply need to learn how to read it correctly. How is this possible? We must develop a personal relationship with God first, ourselves next, and then with others. When we become authentic in our relations, behaviors, and attitudes, God will begin to open up to us on a different level Spiritually.

What is the other level in the Eye of God? It varies from person to person, mission to mission, talent to talent, etc., because we are all different, but trust is one of the most prevalent determining factors in the Kingdom of God. Our Spiritual Fingerprint determines our level, and our ability to learn, grow, and sow determines the progression of our levels of Spirituality. And if we are not trustworthy, we will tend to misuse or abuse our Spiritual Power.

How do we know if we are trustworthy? We must examine the level we are on right now. If we are untrustworthy, it limits us, but more importantly, it does not exempt us. What does this mean? We can work on ourselves to become better by getting an understanding of what God requires of us and the reasons why. Listen, if we attempt to operate on a level we are not designed to be on, we will fail. From a worldly perspective, most would think failing is a bad thing, but from a Spiritual Perspective, failing is not bad at all. Failure gives us an indication, letting us know we need more growth, we must rethink, we should redo, or we need to re-whatever to create a win-win.

From my perspective, failure is the School of Life, helping us to deal with rejection, bondage, traumas, injustices, setbacks, atrocities, as well as all the other negative attributes associated with giving up or settling for defeat. On the other hand, if we bring our emotions under the subjection of the Holy Spirit while setting our mind on understanding, learning, growing, and giving back, our failures give us a golden opportunity to become better and not bitter, increasing our Spiritual Capacity.

According to the Ancient of Days, the essence of who we are is already; we need to TAP IN Spiritually, *As It Pleases God*. How is this possible? We must learn how to truly understand ourselves from the inside out without covering up the lies we tell ourselves.

Spirituality from the Kingdom of Heaven requires us to be authentic. When we are not transparent, we become judgmental, looking for flaws in others when we are living a lie. I am not here to point the finger because we all have our reasons for doing what we do; however, I am here to break the artificial self-imposed barriers keeping us out of the Kingdom or Spiritually Blinded to Divine Purpose.

When we give ourselves the undivided attention we need to deal with our hidden issues, we have less time to insult or assassinate others for being human. Reflecting on the mirror of ourselves from time to time helps in our examination process, building our ability to listen and learn effectively without pointing the finger, turning up our noses, or looking down on others. What is the purpose of doing so? It keeps us from becoming self-righteous, thwarting the Image of God. How do we know if we are thwarting God's Image? Listed below are a few things, but not limited to:

- ☐ Ungodly or Disobedient Character.
- ☐ A Thief.
- ☐ A Liar.
- ☐ A Manipulative Bully or User.
- ☐ Indulging in Utter Chaos and Confusion.

- ☐ A Bad Attitude or Combativeness.
- ☐ Exhibiting Hatefulness.
- ☐ Exhibiting Selfishness and Unappreciativeness.
- ☐ Exhibiting Unforgiveness and Ungratefulness.
- ☐ Setting Traps for the Innocent.
- ☐ Exhibiting Greed.
- ☐ Exhibiting Self-Rightcousness.

Negative character traits are often a dead giveaway of our lack of ability to Tap In Spiritually. Once we genuinely tap in, the Holy Spirit will correct this form of behavior. If the correction is not taking place, it means that we have become Spiritually Blind, Deaf, or Mute. Just so we are clear, this does not mean God will not hear, protect, or anoint us; it means we will stay at a certain Level of Spirituality or we will remain in the Spiritual Classroom a little longer. What does this mean? We are limited in what we can do from a Spiritual Perspective.

For example, if we pray against hatefulness in our child, do we think we can successfully cast it out when we possess the same Spirit? Of course, we can cast it out; however, we need to know where we are casting it to. Being that it came from us, it will come back to us as a Spiritual Transfer. What does this mean? If we cast out something that came from us, it creates a manifestation of the same Spirit, similar to a snowball effect bouncing back and forth, getting worse while gaining momentum to recruit others. Is this real? Absolutely! Unfortunately, this is why we need to repent, replacing the negative with a positive without playing around or overlooking it, period.

In short, Spiritual Oblivion is why we are in this condition today. If we do not get to the root of the essential matters consuming us, we will not endure the wiles of the enemy when we come under Spiritual Attack. When we are too busy trying to figure out who is Spiritually Right or Wrong, the enemy is stealing our children before our eyes. Here is the deal: what really matters is who is Spiritually Effective for the Kingdom of Heaven and who is using the Fruits of the Spirit to lead God's sheep in or out of a

Spiritual Fold or Classroom. We can tiptoe around God's Way to have our own, but in the end, He has the last say.

In my opinion, wasting precious time clogs our ears, drowning out God's Voice and spoiling our fruits to appease the lusts of the flesh, the lusts of the eye, and the pride of life. Doing so inhibits our ability to effectively listen to God, ourselves, and others, creating a domino effect of failed relationships, unions, friendships, etc. When we cannot listen, our inner rebellion affects our ability to exhibit genuine patience, attentiveness, compassion, and readiness. How do we recognize this behavior? It is sometimes found in our pushy, pushy demeanor, our rush, rush attitude, our 'me, me, me' demands, our blaming conduct, our nothing is ever good enough complaints when we are on an outright ego trip, belittling others, and the list goes on.

Due to our open or hidden selfishness, when we do not pay attention, we can develop tunnel vision, blocking our ability to break our self-imposed limitations. By far, this has a way of inhibiting our Spiritual Awareness or Awakening if we are not extremely careful. In the Eye of God, Authentic Spirituality is birthed in our stillness. Often, when we are Spiritually Still, worldly individuals will confuse this with laziness.

In contrast, being still for God is like apples and oranges compared to lackadaisical worldliness. How is this possible? In all due respect, one is a Gateway to God, and the other is a Gateway to Hell.

According to the Ancient of Days, being heard running our mouths is not ideal for the Kingdom of God. Why is there a problem running our mouths too much? We must perfect the art of being heard, loud and clear, without saying one word. How is this possible when talking is a form of communication? Our body language, eye contact, listening skills, Fruits of the Spirit, and Christlike Character speak louder than any spoken word. For instance, when dealing with the Fruits of the Spirit:

- ☐ Love speaks its own language.
- ☐ Joy speaks its own language.

- ☐ Peace speaks its own language.
- ☐ Patience speaks its own language.
- ☐ Kindness speaks its own language.
- ☐ Goodness speaks its own language.
- ☐ Faithfulness speaks its own language.
- ☐ Gentleness speaks its own language.
- ☐ Self-control speaks its own language.

If you do not believe me, try it for 40 days. I promise it will make one a believer, allowing us to fine-tune how we sync our verbal and non-verbal language positively. Unfortunately, these are some of the Spiritual Tools we overlook, circumventing our upright Spiritual Walk with God, *As It Pleases Him*.

How do we recognize when we need Spiritual Silence or a Spiritual Time-Out? Listed below are a few indicators, but not limited to such:

- ☐ When we are uncomfortable being quiet, we talk too much, or we have become a fast-talker.
- ☐ When our mind is all over the place in our moment of silence or solitude.
- ☐ When we cannot sit still, and we are constantly on the go.
- ☐ When we lack humility or exhibit rambunctious behavior.
- ☐ When we are constantly making assumptions without asking fact-finding questions.
- ☐ When we become addicted to drama or chaos.
- ☐ We cannot follow instructions, or we do not listen to anyone.
- ☐ When our flesh is ruling over us, Mentally, Physically, Emotionally, and Spiritually.
- ☐ When we cannot get along with anyone, or we cannot provide a zone of safety or trust.
- ☐ When we pride ourselves on controlling everything, or we are bullies, creating divides.
- ☐ When we feel as if we have to prove ourselves to others, or we take everything personal.

- [ ] When we are battling with envy, jealousy, coveting, pride, or ungratefulness.

Each charactorial flaw can create a layer of unnecessary debris within the psyche. So, we must become cautious about what is clouding our Spiritual Shine or Illumination. We do not want to contend with mixed signals, where our mind is saying one thing, and our heart is saying another. From a Spiritual Perspective, we do not want to create soulish wars that could have been avoided. What makes this so important in the Eye of God? It zaps our ability to focus correctly, solve problems, and maneuver around our present-day issues, causing us to become caught up or turn on ourselves.

Listen, when we are Spiritually Torn, we can become Spiritually Reckless, leaving an open door for the enemy to sift, yoke, or soul tie us, especially if we do not recognize what is taking place or when we are not Spiritually Astute. Therefore, we must recognize when we are wallowing in soulish mush to prevent our souls from becoming hijacked by the enemy.

The bottom line is that when we are weak and vulnerable, we become easy prey. Thus making repentance and prayer of the utmost importance. It enhances our ability to seek God and do a little soul-searching on our behalf, giving us time to understand what is going on with the Mind, Body, Soul, and Spirit. If not, we may fall into a form of inner self-neglect, making it harder to express ourselves, our Gifts, Talents, or Calling. Plus, it also becomes more challenging to develop an authentic Spiritual Relationship without having materialistic ulterior motives. What does this mean? We serve God for the benefits instead of serving Him wholeheartedly, accomplishing His Divine Will or Destiny with or without benefits, simply because it is the right thing to do.

Our Divine Destiny is not predicated on materialism. If our mind is consumed by hoarding, greed, ungratefulness, or coveting, we block ourselves in the pursuit of Destiny. How is this possible, especially when our Divine Destiny belongs to us? It will take us longer to get to where we need to be from a Spiritual Perspective due to the Spiritual Training needed for our Predestined Blueprint. If we avoid it, everything gets delayed because we are repeating the lessons we did not learn the first time around, thus prolonging our Destiny Enriched Provisions or Birthright. As a result, if we are not careful, we can become Spiritually Bankrupt or outright Corrupt through the elements of pretense, deception, or carelessness.

How can we overcome delays? It is best done by repenting first, then praying and listening. However, if we are really yoked, soul-tied, or in bondage, we may need to add a fast to the equation. Although we may not become perfect in hearing God speak to us at first, with time and perseverance, it will come if we focus on using the Word of God as a Divine Tool of reconciliation.

Can God really dialogue with us? Absolutely. The Spiritual Language between each individual is personalized. How is this possible? Before I answer this question, let me counteract it with another one. Who knows us better than we do? It is God Almighty; He knows more about us than we do, and it is through the Holy Spirit that intercession is made on our behalf. Therefore, He knows how to communicate with us...the only issue we are facing in this matter is how to communicate with Him. How do we go about doing so? In the same way that we talk openly with our best friend, we can respectfully communicate with Him in the same way, *As It Pleases Him*.

How can we reduce God to being a friend? A relationship is a relationship, period. In my opinion, it is just a matter of perception or priority. If we need God to be a mother or father, He can be this for us. If we need God to be a sister or brother, He can be this for us. If we need God to be a husband or wife, He can be this for us as well. God can be anything or anyone for us! However, as a word of caution, please do not become the enemy of God. He will definitely make us some form of footstool for something or someone before He breaks us down to the core, bringing shame to us or annihilating our name.

How can we avoid becoming the enemy of God? There are a few ways to do so, but not limited to such:

- ☐ Get rid of the negative distractions blocking our ability to focus.
- ☐ Wholeheartedly use the Fruits of the Spirit with good intentions.
- ☐ Sincerely help others with no strings attached.
- ☐ Seek God's face and not His hand (the benefits).
- ☐ Create a win-win out of everything.
- ☐ Reverse the negatives into positives without passing blame.
- ☐ Keep a Positive Mental Attitude.
- ☐ Become transparent, hopeful, and faithful.
- ☐ We must become usable by listening, learning, and growing positively.
- ☐ We must become obedient and respectful.
- ☐ We must repent, pray, and fast often.
- ☐ We must become shareable, planting good seeds.

Our transformational process is not an overnight one; it is a Spiritual Journey, sifting out the old and ushering in the Spiritual Newness and Awareness of what is Divine. So, it is imperative to work on ourselves positively to bring forth what is already there.

To take possession of our Divine Destiny, *As It Pleases God*, we must be prepared to take ownership. What do we need to take ownership of?

- ☐ We must take ownership of our relationship with the Holy Trinity, which is our Heavenly Father, the Son, and the Holy Spirit.
- ☐ We must take ownership of ourselves, including our thoughts, emotions, and spoken words.
- ☐ We must take ownership of our truth or lies.
- ☐ We must take ownership of our positive or negative fruits.
- ☐ We must take ownership of our perceptions or hidden biases.
- ☐ We must take ownership of our behavior, attitude, and Christlike Character.

- ☐ We must take ownership of our secrets, issues, traumas, or setbacks.
- ☐ We must take ownership of our Gifts, Talents, Creativity, or Calling.
- ☐ We must take ownership of our Divine Destiny or Birthright.
- ☐ We must take ownership of positive or negative foundational principles or traditions.
- ☐ We must take ownership of our ability to share with others.
- ☐ We must take ownership of the teachability, correctability, and discipline of our Mind, Body, Soul, and Spirit.

For change to occur, we must take ownership of whatever it is without passing the buck or pointing the finger. For sure, it is easier to brush things off or pretend as if they do not exist, but we cannot fix what is buried, denied, or sugarcoated. Furthermore, we cannot fully ask the right questions or obtain the correct answers, especially if we lie to God, ourselves, or others about our truth. Although there are things we cannot share with others, we cannot lie to God or ourselves. Yet, we do have the option to plead the 5th to keep our business between God and ourselves if need be.

The Kingdom of God is here for us and through us; therefore, we cannot take it for granted. It is indeed our meal ticket into Heaven if we avail ourselves to the Spiritual Purification needed to open its Floodgates. How do we become purified? There is no set way because we are all different; for this reason, we need the Holy Spirit's presence to seek out what is buried beneath the layers of Spiritual Blockages.

According to the Heavenly of Heavens, our blockages will not be the same as the next person's due to our conditioning, traumas, background, biases, etc. For this reason, we need the Holy Spirit to illuminate the hidden crevices of potential defeat or open doors we left for the enemy to throw us under the bus. And then, we need the Blood of Jesus to cover us as Spiritual Atonement to gain Spiritual Insight, *As It Pleases God*, with the *Heavenly Linguistics* to put the enemy to boot.

Chapter 3

SPIRITUAL INSIGHT

God's ultimate desire is to help us develop our *Spiritual Insight* and Spiritual Learning capabilities. What is this? It is a sudden revelation of how to solve problems, issues, and situations without allowing anxiety or fear to consume us. It is through the use of our Spiritual Instincts outside of the use of our worldly instincts. Shouldn't we use both of them? Yes, we should; however, we must learn how to use them correctly. Believe it or not, our worldly instincts leave room for speculations, biases, and assumptions. Yet, with our Spiritual Instincts, we can see beyond the natural into the Supernatural, giving us a bird's eye view from all perspectives with a Divine Compass.

How do we obtain a Divine Compass with Spiritual Insight? Through the use of our *Spirit to Spirit* Relationship via the Holy Trinity (Father, Son, and Holy Spirit) for Divine Revelation, when used with the Fruits of the Spirit and Christlike Character, with proper documentation. What if we do not document? We become limited in the Eye of God, becoming a stepping stone instead of a Cornerstone, *As It Pleases God*. Really? Yes, really!

Clearly, God will use anyone or anything to accomplish His Divine Will; however, during our use, He wants our Testaments to become Testimonies for others. More importantly, according to the Heavenly of Heavens, the best way to gain Divine Insight is to give it, activating the Law of Reciprocity to open up the Spiritual Floodgates of Divine Wisdom, Secrets, and Treasures. Here is the

Spiritual Seal hidden in plain sight: *"Write the vision And make it plain on tablets, That he may run who reads it. For the vision is yet for an appointed time; But at the end it will speak, and it will not lie. Though it tarries, wait for it; Because it will surely come, It will not tarry."* Habakkuk 2:2-3.

Our inner man knows and understands more than we give it credit for; therefore, we must develop a way to sync ourselves back to God's original design, *As It Pleases Him*. How is this possible? It will take a little Spiritual Training to understand the Nudges and Voice of God or the Holy Spirit to prune the negative inner chatter by unconditioning our conditions. Most of what we are dealing with today is based upon what we have been conditioned to think, say, and become, positively or negatively.

I am not here to judge anyone's home training, period. It has appropriately positioned one to be in the right place at the right time to read this book right now. But more importantly, I am merely the Spiritual Messenger of the Good News. Now, to step up to the next level in our Spirituality, we must unlearn, relearn, or disengage specific characteristics associated with keeping us from the Kingdom of Heaven and its Heavenly Benefits.

When in the learning process or the Spiritual Classroom of God, we are required to think openly. Limited thinking places us in boxes we should not be in, or it limits our problem-solving capabilities, which also limits our instincts by default. Spiritually, this is how we lose touch with ourselves and God to the highest degree, causing unhealthy or unfruitful habits, strongholds, soul ties, or outright becoming stuck in a rut or pimping God.

Bottom line, convergent thinking is not going to get it because God is not a one-way God; He has many ways of doing what He does, through whomever He desires and however. So, it is imperative to open our minds to becoming divergent in our way of thinking. What is this? It is innovative thinking with a positively guarded open mind.

Why do we need to become divergent in our way of thinking? God has designed us as Creative Beings, and if we have a desire to break open the Vault of Greatness, we must become Spiritually Creative without becoming limited in our process of good, positive, and fruitful thoughts and habits. All we need to do is keep the negative, evil, hateful, and unfruitful thoughts and habits at bay. If not, we can easily give way to our lusts, emotions, habits, or traumas, so be careful. What is the reason for such caution? We can become Spiritually Blind, Deaf, or Mute if we misuse our minds to create or enforce ill will or operate in disobedience.

What is the purpose of having our Spiritual Eyes, Ears, and Mouth open to God? When God has us to look at something or someone, we need to see it from His Perspective, not ours. We must begin to trust the Spiritual Algorithms of God, *As It Pleases Him.*

When God says move, we need to move, knowing He is guiding our every footstep. When He says hold up, we need to patiently step into a holding pattern, regardless of who is trying to bully us. When He says fold, we need to fold it without grieving or wallowing too long, knowing all things will work together for our good. When God gives us a word, we must speak it, similar to what I am doing now. When God sends us on a Spiritual Mission or places us in Purpose on purpose, we do not have to be Creatively Perfect or remember every detail regarding it.

The Holy Spirit is designed to help, train, and guide us, leaving Spiritual Breadcrumbs for us to follow. We simply need to get out of our own way, especially when utilizing our Spiritual Gifts, Creativity, or Talents.

If we move to our own algorithms, we can easily become functionally fixed on having and doing things our way, limiting our Creative Capacity to expand our minds beyond our selfish patterns or conditioning. Unfortunately, this is another reason why some people play mind games, hijacking others' ideas to cover up their functionally fixed mindset of surface-level self-creativity, causing us to psychoanalyze based on our limits. The truth of the matter is that we all have a level of uniqueness from a Spiritual Perspective as it relates to our Divine Destiny or Blueprint. If we do not recognize it, it becomes difficult to tap into our CREATIVE FORCES of Greatness, break our self-imposed limitations, or come to terms with how we truly feel about ourselves from the inside out.

How can we revamp our algorithm to a more Spiritual one? We must positively shift our perspective with the Fruits of the Spirit at the forefront. Surely, it determines our in-look (view from within) and our outlook about God, self, others, and life, providing the ability to properly examine ourselves thoroughly without expecting our validity to come from people. When we maintain the proper perspectives with God at the forefront, we do not have to depend upon worldly validation of our *Spiritual Insight* or *Spiritual Learning* capabilities.

If we can get the negative projecting people out of our heads, we are better able to maximize our Creative Genius. How is this possible? We can ask ourselves open-ended questions without having the opinions of others to taint our Divine Q&A Session being led by the Holy Spirit. Listen, the way we question ourselves from a Creative Perspective should contain multiple documented answers to expand our thought or building process. Whereas, if we ask ourselves closed-ended questions, such as the 'yes' or 'no' questions, it invokes limits without any form of additional elaboration.

The goal is to develop a zone of Spiritual Elaboration and Collaboration where documentation is a must. When we develop the '*mind to pen*' and the '*pen to paper*' mentality, we can project and capture our thoughts consistently if used properly. From me, I call this process my '*Spiritual Jingle*,' which is a process of getting our mind to think Supernaturally, capturing what it is saying without any form of judgment. Why do we need to do this? It remains optional because we all have free will. If one decides to use this method, it is Spiritual Training Wheels for the Mind, Body, Soul, and Spirit, balancing and conditioning us to produce information outside of formal or worldly training. Does it work? Absolutely...if it did not, one would not be reading this book right now.

When developing our Spiritual Training Wheels, the elaboration process helps us to overcome a few open or hidden stages in life, such as:

- ☐ The Searching Phase.
- ☐ The Isolation Phase.
- ☐ The Shamefulness Phase.
- ☐ The Doubting Phase.

- ☐ The Guilt Phase.
- ☐ The Confusion Phase.
- ☐ The Identity Crisis Phase.
- ☐ The Victim Phase.
- ☐ The Betrayal Phase.
- ☐ The Acceptance Phase.
- ☐ The Intimacy Phase.
- ☐ The Freedom Phase.

We are all going to experience life, and while going through it, it is always best to equip ourselves with the Spiritual Tools to help or benefit us along the way.

When we have an understanding, we are better able to seek a viable solution, as long as we do not ask ourselves closed-ended questions, blocking the elaboration process. Why is this process so important? Most often, all of the answers we seek to our questions are already within; we simply need to search for them honestly by doing a query on ourselves to get to the root of whatever it is.

If our queries are not dealt with accordingly, one will find themselves battling for their mental stability while discrediting or pointing the finger at others for theirs. Why would this become problematic in the Eye of God? If we are unsure, if we are not okay with not having the answers, or if we are not able to detect our solutional threshold of the answers already presented from within, we will subconsciously want others to feel the same way as well. Is this Godly? No, it is not; however, it is real! Frankly, this is why we need the Fruits of the Spirit to assist us in balancing our Mental, Physical, Emotional, and Spiritual states of being while building Christlike Character, *As It Pleases God.*

When we overlook the Fruits of the Spirit's developmental process, we will find that our ability to be at peace with God, ourselves, and others will become problematic. In so many words, inner peace will cease to exist within the pit of our soul, which will invoke known and unknown battles from within.

Developing a problematic size assessment from a Spiritual Perspective helps us determine the level of warfare needed to deal with the issues at hand. What does this mean? If we have a small problem, such as someone not taking out the trash, it only requires us to address the issue without engaging in a full-blown Spiritual Battle.

On the other hand, if we have become ungodly soul-tied to something or someone, it may require a more advanced warfare level to break the ties. But more importantly, we must know the difference to prevent ourselves from going overboard or becoming exhausted with minor issues in the Eye of God! Why should we sever ungodly soul ties? We will have more time to spend on developing Spiritual Fruits with proven results, *As It Pleases God*, to establish conducive relations. Listed below are a few reasons to develop our Spiritual Fruits, but not limited to such:

- It helps us to *Love* without any strings attached or going overboard.
- It helps us to become *Joyful* from within amid chaos.
- It helps us to be at *Peace* with ourselves, accepting ourselves for who we are.
- It helps us to remain *Patient* when we are in a holding pattern of life.
- It helps us to be *Kind* to those who despitefully use us or who are unkind to us.
- It helps us do *Good* to others when they are mean, nasty, wayward, hateful, and cruel.
- It helps us to remain *Faithful* in the midst of trying or desperate times.
- It helps us to become *Gentle* in our thoughts, actions, words, touch, and demeanor.
- It helps us to develop *Self-Control* in knowing when to respond and when not to, when to do and when not to, or when to hold and when to fold.

What is the purpose of utilizing our Spiritual Fruits? It creates respect, period. If we bump into blatantly disrespectful people, we must raise an eyebrow at where they are getting their fruits. By far, this is how we become deceived into thinking someone would treat our fruits better than they treat their own. So, we must exercise extreme caution when creating idols out of humans or golden calves, especially when one's behavior is not Christlike, cruel, evil, sifting, degrading, or outright atrocious with an unguarded tongue.

We can beat around the bush when it comes down to the Fruits of the Spirit and their uses. However, we cannot deny the fact that we are positively moved inwardly, especially when they are exhibited toward us, regardless of how hard we pretend to be. Why does this happen? Because we already possess our Spiritual Fruits, they are just buried or have become rotten underneath layers of hurt, trauma, rejection, failure, conditioning, and the list goes on with negative attributes. But by all means, it does not mean we have to give in to the wrong types of fruits, nor does it mean we should lose our ability to respect God, ourselves, and others.

As we move on, keep in mind that if we desire *Spiritual Insight*, we must respect the process of receiving it. If we disrespect God, do we think He will open a stream of Divine Wisdom to us? Of course not, because we may become careless with it. Yet, we can indeed obtain knowledge, skills, and know-how outside of Him. What is the difference? Divine Wisdom is a Direct Connection to and from the Holy Trinity (The Father, Son, and Holy Spirit).

The other means of getting information can come from anything, anyone, or anyhow. Yet, if we are receiving some form of presumable wisdom outside of the Holy Trinity, it is a familiar Spirit. So, be very careful when taking or gleaning information in such a manner. Why should we be careful as Believers? Dealing with familiar Spirits comes with a price, and trust me, it is not free! Plus, it will cause us to overgeneralize or overrationalize the Kingdom of Heaven. How so? By making negative statements such as:

- ☐ It does not take all of that.

- ☐ The Bible contradicts itself.
- ☐ All Pastors are thieves.
- ☐ Christians are a bunch of hypocrites.
- ☐ The Church is evil.
- ☐ The Church is all about money.
- ☐ Christians are weak.
- ☐ Christians are gullible.
- ☐ The Church is corruptible.
- ☐ The Church cannot do anything for us.
- ☐ The Church is a business.
- ☐ The Church is brainwashing people.
- ☐ Everyone is trying to be an expert on God or the Bible.

One cannot scrape the surface of the negative projections being cast over the Kingdom of God. Personally, I have heard some mind-boggling statements about Christians and the Church from those who have been scorned in some way. Yet, it does not change the fact that we must set a guard over our mouths, preserving ourselves as well as our Bloodline.

Listen, getting caught up in a negative rampage about the Kingdom is not wise under any circumstances. Why should we avoid getting caught up? God is the Divine Creator of all things, including the oxygen we are breathing. If He withdrew His Oxygenated Hand from us, we would cease to exist. Therefore, we should never get too high-minded, thinking we have arrived. God has a way of humbling us when we least expect it.

Just so we are clear, it is not our responsibility to judge others, especially when we are speculating or not walking a straight and narrow path with God or our Purpose. Once again, we do not know what God is doing with or through someone; therefore, it is best to save ourselves from negatively projecting lies, ill will, or whatever over someone or the Church.

If we are not extremely careful, we can inadvertently cast the same negative projection over our lives or Bloodline. How is this possible? Unjustifiable judgments or projections we set in motion can backfire if we come against a Spiritual Elite. What does this mean? If God has chosen someone for a specific Spiritual Mission, and this person is in proper alignment with their Destiny, we do not want to contend with this person negatively. When a person is in Purpose on purpose, *As It Pleases God*, we can become an enemy of God due to their Spiritual Covering or Divine Protection.

Then again, if it is someone who is not even close to doing what they were called to do for the Kingdom, God will shut them down, period! The only time God will not shut them down is when He is using them to become a footstool to bless, train, teach, correct, or discipline the Chosen Elect, preparing them to become the Cornerstone of Greatness or fill a need for the Greater Good.

What do our needs have to do with our *Spiritual Insight*? In the Eye of God, we all have human needs, even if we do not recognize them or outright deny them. Listed below are a few, but not limited to such:

- ☐ Physiological needs: Food, water, shelter, and other basic necessities required for survival.
- ☐ Safety needs: The need for security, stability, and protection from hurt, harm, or danger.
- ☐ Love and belonging needs: The need for social interaction, connection, love, and intimacy.
- ☐ Self-actualization needs: The need for personal growth, achieving one's full potential, and self-fulfillment.
- ☐ Creativity needs: The need for creative expression, exploration, expansion, and innovation.
- ☐ Autonomy needs: The need for independence, control, free will, and freedom.
- ☐ Purpose needs: The need for meaning, direction, and a sense of purpose.
- ☐ Competence needs: The need for mastery, skill, and achievement.
- ☐ Trust needs: The need for faith, honesty, respect, hope, and transparency.
- ☐ Learning needs: The need for knowledge, understanding, articulation, wisdom, and gleaning.

- ☐ Health needs: The need for Mental, Physical, and Emotional health, wellness, and self-care.
- ☐ Spiritual needs: The need for a *Spirit to Spirit* Relational Connection to our Heavenly Father.

What is the purpose of knowing about our needs? Our Spiritual Treasures and Insights are often hidden within them. So, if we do not know what they are or are not, we CANNOT truly establish Spiritual Excellence, *As It Pleases God*. Conversely, when a need is not fulfilled, deprivation can occur, leading to thirst, hunger, desire, longing, desperation, or void. Therefore, to *Fix Our Crown* properly, we must understand the needs associated with securing it, *As It Pleases God*. Here is what we must know: "*We have this treasure in earthen vessels, that the excellence of the power may be of God and not of us.*" Corinthians 4:7.

Chapter 4

FIX YOUR CROWN

Contrary to what most believe, our Religious beliefs are NOT genetically inherited; however, Blessings, Birthrights, and Curses remain in our Bloodline until they run their course or are broken. What does this mean? It means that Religion is a cultured, conditioned, or influenced belief of whatever we relate back to. Spiritually Speaking, regardless of what we think or believe, we have free will to choose or change *How, What, When, Where*, and with *Whom* to believe, positively or negatively.

Now, based upon the choices we make as they relate to our Religious Practices, it produces Blessings, Birthrights, and Curses based upon our beliefs, actions, reactions, attitudes, and the list goes on, passing on its Seasonal Cycle into our Bloodline in the form of blessed, rotten, or cursed fruits. For this reason, it is always best to develop a Spiritual Relationship with our Heavenly Father, the Son, and the Holy Spirit. Doing so helps to preserve our Bloodline, develop Christlike Character, and learn how to properly use the Fruits of the Spirit as benefits to assist us on our Spiritual Journey. In addition, listed below are a few more Spiritual Principles to help us along the way.

- ☐ We must become aware of the language we speak on a moment-by-moment basis, be it worldly or Spiritual.

- ☐ We must avoid setting intentional traps to Mentally, Physically, Emotionally, or Spiritually sink ourselves or others.
- ☐ We must be willing to grow, change, and become trustworthy in our thoughts, desires, actions, and reactions.
- ☐ We must respectfully put people, places, and things into their proper perspective without fault-finding or invoking the negative.
- ☐ We must master the ability to remain calm and patient without losing our cool. If one needs to meditate to remain calm, please do not hesitate to do so.
- ☐ We must hone in on changing our perspective regarding distractions and setbacks to create a win-win.
- ☐ We must be willing to ask fact-finding questions to get to the root of our truth.
- ☐ We must become crystal clear about what we are doing, saying, and becoming.
- ☐ We must face our fears, problems, and setbacks with an openness to learn, grow, and sow.
- ☐ We must train our minds to restructure bad news into good, fruitful, and positive Good News.
- ☐ We must regraft or refocus our thought thermostat to remain in an upright direction, focused on doing the right thing and literally counting our Blessings. If we have to use our fingers and toes to count our Blessings, then so be it!
- ☐ We must train ourselves to lean toward problem-solving instead of worry-solving by grounding ourselves in Biblical

Truths and Affirmations while engaging in random acts of kindness.

Why do we need Spiritual Principles? It serves as a Spiritual Guide or Tool to help us become interdependent in doing our part as it relates to the upkeep of our Spiritual Vessel. Also, following Godly, Positive, and Fruitful Principles helps us properly align ourselves, squashing negative thoughts, beliefs, or actions. How is this possible? Through counteracting inconsistent soulish negativity with positive proactiveness. By doing so, it subconsciously brings our Mind, Body, Soul, and Spirit into alignment, ushering in Character Consistency.

Whether we are surface acting (faking it) or deep acting (making a serious attempt to do right), consistency is a must in the Kingdom to ensure we can put away any form of malice, unforgiveness, coveting, jealousy, envy, or pride. What does this mean? It means that we are NOT all over the place Mentally, Physically, Emotionally, and Spiritually, experiencing erratic behaviors, thoughts, attitudes, etc., with all types of conflicting contradictions, rationalizations, or justifications. In layman's terms, this is when our mind is saying one thing, our heart is saying another, and our mouth contradicts all the above.

For the Kingdom of God, He requires Genuine Acting individuals who will put their hidden biases aside to embrace their Divine Purpose with a true Labor of Love. The Kingdom Mindset is not for those who are hell-bent on doing things their way. As a Spiritual Vessel, we need to understand a few things:

- ☐ We need to identify problems without avoiding, overlooking, or exaggerating them.

- ☐ We need to look for solutions without sugar-coating the truth.

- ☐ We need to know how to gain Biblical Insight, understanding whatever it is from God's point of view.

- ☐ We need to understand the power of having free will to change or regraft our thoughts, behaviors, words, and emotions for the better.

- ☐ We must understand that everyone is entitled to their own opinion.

- ☐ We must exhibit unconditional positive regard for those we come in contact with, combating the natural tendency to become selfish, disrespectful, or judgmental.

- ☐ We must understand that our personal drive must incorporate developing and maintaining a Positive Mental Attitude.

- ☐ We must understand that in order to change our mindset positively, we must change our perceptions to incorporate lessons, strategies, and concepts of a win-win, not a defeat.

- ☐ We must have continuous Spiritual Reinforcement of our Spiritual Fruits and Christlike Character to penetrate man's heart and become Spiritually Effective in the Kingdom.

- ☐ We must have time alone to pray and meditate to relieve the known and unknown stressors or negative energy, preventing us from getting uptight, stressed, or anxious.

- ☐ We must understand that humility is a prerequisite for gaining Spiritual Insight into the Kingdom of Heaven.

- ☐ We must be willing to adjust our selfish vision or limiting beliefs to accommodate a Higher Vision of our Divine Destiny as the Ultimate Rewards of our Faith.

Contrary to what most believe, the Kingdom of Heaven has benefits and rewards that money cannot buy. Yet, we will most often not recognize the need for these types of rewards until we become desperate, soul-tied, yoked, or sifted. Why must it get to this point for Believers? The value is not established until it has been proven to work on our behalf. According to 1 Corinthians 9:24-25, here is what we must know: *"Do you not know that those who run in a race all run, but one receives the prize? Run in such a way that you may obtain it. And everyone who competes for the prize is temperate in all things. Now they do it to obtain a perishable crown, be we for an imperishable crown."*

From my perspective, earthly rewards are great, and I am totally grateful for everything; however, the Rewards of the Kingdom are second to none. We have been conditioned to place value in things that are fleeting, growing old, or wearing out, overlooking the fact that there is more to life hidden right before our very eyes in Earthen Vessels. Let me interject 2 Corinthians 4:7: *"But we have this treasure in Earthen Vessels, that the excellence of the Power may be of God and not of us."* But, hold on a moment, let us take this a little further, *"Even if our gospel is veiled, it is veiled to those who are perishing, whose minds the god of this age has blinded, who do not believe, lest the light of the gospel of the Glory of Christ, who is the image of God, should shine on them."* 2 Corinthians 4:3-4.

If we desire to become unveiled, I am required to shed light on the Treasures and Rewards of the Kingdom, cutting through the manipulative hogwash. Why must we cut through the mess as Believers? The Spiritual Reshaping we need is already within us; we simply need to know it. How is it possible to already possess what we need in Earthen Vessel? The Spiritual Anointing I possess is available to all; we must cut through the blinding red tape.

According to the Ancient of Days, we are all formed from the Dust of the Earth, making our Earthen Vessels pliable, especially if we avail ourselves to the Spiritual Molding process when under heat or when we get a little muddy. From a Spiritual Perspective, this does not deface our Hidden Greatness; in all actuality, it is by far the perfecting or training process used to extract Heavenly Treasures.

What are the Treasurable Rewards of the Kingdom? There are many; however, I will point out a few to jumpstart our Spiritual Elevation, but not limited to such:

- ☐ We have a Father in Heaven who will never leave, forsake, abuse, or use us.
- ☐ The Spiritual Guidance and Comforting of the Holy Spirit.
- ☐ The use of the Blood of Jesus as a sacrifice for our sins.
- ☐ The Fruits of the Spirit.
- ☐ Grace, Mercy, and Forgiveness.
- ☐ Spiritual Covering, Power, Authority, and Protection.
- ☐ The Whole Armor of God.
- ☐ The Breath of Life and Living Water.
- ☐ The Gifts of the Spirit.
- ☐ Treasures in Heaven of our Eternal Inheritance.

We can tiptoe around our Spiritual Treasures, or we can take possession of what rightly belongs to us. In my opinion, we have come too far to leave our Birthrights and Promises of God on the table for those who have not put in the work. As it relates to our Divine Mission, we have two options:

- ☐ Build the Kingdom of God.
- ☐ Tear down the Kingdom of God.

If one does not believe in having a Divine Foundation or our Spiritual Ordination, we must read 1 Peter 1:1-25 to settle the matter once and for all. This Chapter changed my life, and I am convinced it will impact the lives of all. Moreover, we must decide which side of the fence we are leaning toward. Why must we know whose side we are on as Believers? It determines if we are an asset or a liability to the Kingdom of Heaven.

What is the purpose of deciding on the Kingdom? It helps to avoid collateral damage, minimize the misuse of Kingdom Principles, and circumvent generational curses. Just so we are clear, this does not mean we have to be 100% perfect; we simply need to make a willing decision of our intent regardless of our strengths or weaknesses, good or bad, right or wrong, etc. God can use them all because our treasures are often hidden in our weaknesses, wrongs, handicaps, struggles, traumas, and the list goes on. Therefore, we should never count ourselves out before making an outright attempt to correct the correctable or maximize the minimized.

Contrary to popular belief, our past is NOT set in stone if we master the ability to change how we perceive it positively. How is this possible? Our minds can create images to build and destroy us; however, if we alter the images or memories we are playing back to ourselves, we will better understand the Power of the Mind and how well it can create whatever it wants. If we do not learn how to reel our thoughts in or revise our thought patterns positively, our past images will overshadow our Kingdom Treasures. How is this possible? We will not recognize them when we see them due to Spiritual Blindness, Deafness, or Muteness. Why am I saying all of this? It is because if I had listened to my naysayers without reframing my mindset toward Godly Principles, you would not be reading this book right now. What is more, I would not be able to reach inside the soul of man with such conviction, passion, and steadfast clarity.

This book is one of my Treasurable Givebacks to the Kingdom to ensure we can obtain our Heavenly Crowns rightfully due to us. What does this mean? *"By the God of your father who will help you, And by the Almighty who will bless you With blessings of heaven above, Blessings of the deep that lies beneath, Blessings of the breasts and of the womb. The blessings of your father have excelled the blessings of my ancestors, up to the utmost bound of the everlasting hills. They shall be on the head of Joseph, And on the crown of the head of him who was separate from his brothers."* Genesis 49:25-26. Now, with our Treasurable Rewards come five Heavenly Crowns:

- ☐ **Imperishable Crown.** *"To an inheritance incorruptible and undefiled and that does not fade away, reserved in Heaven for you, who are kept by the Power of God through faith for salvation ready to be revealed in the last time."* 1 Peter 1:4-5.

- ☐ **Crown of Rejoicing.** *"For what is our hope, or joy, or Crown of Rejoicing? Is it not even you in the presence of our Lord Jesus Christ at His coming? For you are our glory and joy."* 1 Thessalonians 2:19-20.

- ☐ **Crown of Righteousness.** *"Finally, there is laid up for me the Crown of Righteousness, which the Lord the righteous Judge, will give to me on that Day, and not to me only but also to all who have loved His appearing."* 2 Timothy 4:8.

- ☐ **Crown of Glory.** *"When the Chief Shepherd appears, you will receive the Crown of Glory that does not fade away."* 1 Peter 5:4.

- ☐ **Crown of Life.** *"Do not fear any of those things which you are to suffer. Indeed, the devil is about to throw some of you into prison, that you may be tested, and you will have tribulations ten days. Be faithful until death, and I will give you the Crown of Life."* Revelation 2:10.

When we speak about Crowns, we usually associate them with the Crown of Success. Meanwhile, the appearance of success does not necessarily mean Spiritual Success, *As It Pleases God.* Why is ordinary success different from Divine Success? If we are not using our Gifts, Talents, Calling, or Creativity, or we are outright out of Purpose, we only fool ourselves about real success.

Success in the eyes of man is totally different from what it means in the Eye of God. If we have to convince others with worldly tangibilities without having God in the equation, more than likely, we do not feel successful from the pit of our souls, and we cannot tell anyone about this annoying void. As a result of this secret insecurity, it invokes pride, coveting, envy, jealousy, control, judging, criticizing, and the list goes on with negative character traits to prove our worthiness.

How can we reverse the void from within? For starters, please understand Exodus 39:30: *"Then they made the plate of the holy crown of pure gold, and wrote on it an inscription like the engraving of a signet: HOLINESS TO THE LORD."* If we stamp this statement on the Breastplate of our Mind, Body, Soul, and Spirit in all we do, say, and become, it becomes the Anointing Oil of Distinction. How is this possible? We already possess what we need, including our CROWN, according to Psalm 8:5: *"For You have made him a little lower than the angels, and You have crowned him with glory and honor."* I know this seems far-fetched to most, rest assured, it is as real as the oxygen we are breathing right now. Listed below are a few ways to do our part in the Anointing Process, but not limited to such:

- ☐ We must become true to ourselves.
- ☐ We must become grateful and non-judgmental.
- ☐ We must change our focus to Kingdom Principles.
- ☐ We must repent of any deception or unrighteousness.
- ☐ We must revamp our negative traits into positive ones.
- ☐ We must begin exhibiting the Fruits of the Spirit.
- ☐ We must begin to unveil our Gifts, Talents, or Creativity.
- ☐ We must stop using material possessions to manipulate, control, or bully others.
- ☐ We must focus on doing the right thing and Spiritually Tilling our own ground, *As It Pleases God*.
- ☐ We must become willing to teach, mentor, motivate, and encourage others.
- ☐ We must begin to share freely with others.
- ☐ We must recognize God as being our Source.

We all have a desire to belong, we have a longing to be recognized, we all want to be respected, and we also have a need to achieve. If we are clueless about fulfilling these desires or how to tap into our

Gifts, Talents, Creativity, or Calling, we will settle for worldly means of doing so. Or, we may beat down or not support those who seemingly have the upper hand in doing so. Well, either way, all is not lost. Spiritual Reformation is here to set the record straight on how to allow the Lamp under our feet to shine, guiding our every footstep.

How can we lose our Spiritual Crown? The first way to lose our Crown is not realizing we have one, forfeiting our Birthright due to some form of Spiritual Blindness, Deafness, or Muteness. Now, for the second way, I am going to take it to scripture: *"He made a pit and dug it out, and has fallen into the ditch which he made. His trouble shall return upon his own head, and his violent dealing shall come down on his own crown."* Psalm 7:16.

Just so we are crystal clear, I am not here to condemn anyone; I am only here to empower another's Crown. *"For You meet him with the blessings of goodness; You set a crown of pure gold upon his head. He asked life from You, and You gave it to him—Length of days forever and ever."* Psalm 21:3-4. If we reach beyond our self-imposed limitations using the Fruits of the Spirit as our Spiritual Behavioral Guide, we can change the trajectory of our lives for the better. How is this possible? According to scripture, if *"You crown the year with Your goodness, and Your paths drip with abundance."* Psalm 65:11.

What are the benefits of having a Spiritual Crown? Once again, I must align this with scripture: *"Bless the LORD, O my soul, and forget not all His benefits: Who forgives all your iniquities, Who heals all your diseases, Who redeems your life from destruction, Who crowns you with loving-kindness and tender mercies, Who satisfies your mouth with good things, So that your youth is renewed like the eagle's. The LORD executes righteousness and justice for all who are oppressed."* Psalm 103:2-6.

What else can our Spiritual Crown do for us, *As It Pleased God?* *"There I will make the horn of David grow; I will prepare a lamp for My Anointed. His enemies I will clothe with shame, but upon Himself His crown shall flourish."* Psalm 132:17-18. Therefore, this creates a Spiritual Reformation for the Kingdom of Heaven.

Chapter 5

SPIRITUAL LAMPSTAND

The Lamp of Light comes with the Spiritual Oil needed to keep it lit, but if we think our oil is potent enough to stave off the wiles of the enemy, we are sadly mistaken. Why are we mistaken as Believers, especially when Salvation is for us? God is the Head Chief in charge, and if we dare to think we can take the Creator out of the equation, we trip ourselves up from the inside out. It does not matter what the world has to say; here is what we need to know to enable our *Spiritual Lampstands* to shine brightly: *"The lamp of the body is the eye. If therefore your eye is good, your whole body will be full of light. But if your eye is bad, your whole body will be full of darkness. If therefore the light that is in you is darkness, how great is that darkness!"* Matthew 6:22-23.

Our Spiritual Eye (Spiritual Consciousness) is the window to the soul, aligning us with our Spiritual Conscience. Meanwhile, our worldly eye (worldly consciousness) aligns us with our worldliness through the lusts of the flesh, the lusts of the eye, and the pride of life. Although God has given us everything we need to accomplish our Divine Mission, we also need Spiritual Guidance to illuminate our path, and we must become humble to get it. Here is what Matthew 5:14-16 says about this: *"You are the light of the world. A city that is set on a hill cannot be hidden. Nor do they light a lamp and put it under a basket, but on a lampstand, and it gives light to all who are in the house. Let your light so shine before men, that they may see your good works and glorify your Father in Heaven."*

How do we get started on our path to Spiritual Illumination? According to scripture, *"The entrance of Your words gives light; It gives understanding to the simple."* We cannot illuminate the soul of another by offending or provoking them. They will develop a deaf ear, block us mentally, or break us down emotionally by lashing out with hate or spite. Therefore, we must master the ability to speak or minister to the weary without invoking offense or feelings of unworthiness.

The next step is to get an understanding of the Light of God, ourselves, and others. What does this mean? We must focus on the good without pointing out the bad as a form of crucifixion. How can we avoid doing so? We must become an example without making others feel unworthy. *"No one, when he has lit a lamp, covers it with a vessel or puts it under a bed, but sets it on a lampstand, that those who enter may see the light."* Luke 8:16.

Our worthship is crucial to the Kingdom, and so is the worthship of another. Here is what 1 Peter 2:9-10 tells us: *"But you are a chosen generation, a royal priesthood, a holy nation, His own special people, that you may proclaim the praises of Him who called you out of darkness into His marvelous light; who once were not a people but are now the people of God, who had not obtained mercy but now have obtained mercy."* By far, mercy has a way of causing our light to shine bright in the eyes of those who are Spiritually Blind. If we compassionately take them by the hand, exhibiting the Fruits of the Spirit without having an ulterior motive, we can penetrate to the core of their being.

What if we do not operate according to Kingdom Principles? We have free will to do whatever we like, but our Spiritual Light will grow dim. Here is what Revelation 2:4-5 advises: *"Nevertheless I have this against you, that you have left your first love. Remember therefore from where you have fallen; repent and do the first works, or else I will come to you quickly and remove your lampstand from its place—unless you repent."*

Here are the Spiritual Declarations hidden in the Book of Revelation.

- ☐ *"He who has an ear, let him hear what the Spirit says to the churches. To him who overcomes, I will give to eat from the Tree of Life, which is in the midst of the Paradise of God."* Revelation 2:7.

- ☐ "He who has an ear, let him hear what the Spirit says to the churches. He who overcomes shall not be hurt by the second death." Revelation 2:11.

- ☐ "He who has an ear, let him hear what the Spirit says to the churches. To him who overcomes I will give some of the hidden manna to eat. And I will give him a white stone, and on the stone a new name written which no one knows except him who receives it." Revelation 2:17.

- ☐ "And he who overcomes, and keeps My works until the end, to him I will give power over the nations—He shall rule them with a rod of iron; they shall be dashed to pieces like the potter's vessels'—as I also have received from My Father; and I will give him the morning star. He who has an ear, let him hear what the Spirit says to the churches." Revelation 2:26-29.

- ☐ "Be watchful, and strengthen the things which remain, that are ready to die, for I have not found your works perfect before God. Remember therefore how you have received and heard; hold fast and repent. Therefore if you will not watch, I will come upon you as a thief, and you will not know what hour I will come upon you. You have a few names even in Sardis who have not defiled their garments; and they shall walk with Me in white, for they are worthy. He who overcomes shall be clothed in white garments, and I will not blot out his name from the Book of Life; but I will confess his name before My Father and before His angels. He who has an ear, let him hear what the Spirit says to the churches." Revelation 3:2-6.

- ☐ "Because you have kept My command to persevere, I also will keep you from the hour of trial which shall come upon the whole world, to test those who dwell on the earth. Behold, I am coming quickly! Hold fast what you have, that no one may take your crown. He who overcomes, I will make him a pillar in the temple of My God, and he shall go out no more. *I will write on him the name of My God and the name of the city of My God, the New Jerusalem, which comes down out of heaven from My God. And I will write on him My new name. He who has an ear, let him hear what the Spirit says to the churches."* Revelation 3:10-13.

☐ *"Behold, I stand at the door and knock. If anyone hears My voice and opens the door, I will come in to him and dine with him, and he with Me. To him who overcomes I will grant to sit with Me on My throne, as I also overcame and sat down with My Father on His throne. He who has an ear, let him hear what the Spirit says to the churches."* Revelation 3:20-22.

Our *Spiritual Lampstands* are more powerful than we think, but one would never want to be removed from the Divine Table, especially in a time such as this. So, it is imperative to open our Spiritual Ears to hear the Voice of God when dealing with our Spiritual Illumination. We must understand the Elements of the Spirit to ensure we do not miss the mark or misinterpret what is being said.

How can Spiritual Illumination help us? Here is what Revelation 3:7-8 says to us: "*And to the angel of the church in Philadelphia write, These things says He who is holy, He who is true, He who has the key of David, He who opens and no one shuts, and shuts and no one opens: I know your works. See, I have set before you an open door, and no one can shut it; for you have a little strength, have kept My word, and have not denied My name.*"

In addition, if we practice lighting our Spiritual Lamp daily through the conscious use of the Fruits of the Spirit, it will help us become accustomed to exhibiting Christlike Character Traits. What does this mean? Suppose we practice or incorporate new positive behaviors and thoughts in our daily living. In this case, we can regraft negative unconscious character traits or desires of immorality, especially if we become consistent while getting a proper understanding of 'Why' we are doing what we do. If not, we can become sifted, losing our seat due to lovelessness, unjustified persecution of the weary, overzealous compromise, and materialistic corruptibility, hindering our faithfulness to the Kingdom.

Just so we are clear, the Spiritual Messengers of Light, in such a time as this, are swift in pursuing righteousness and the hidden truths and mysteries of the Kingdom to ensure their feet and tongue do not slip. They are also quick to examine themselves, repenting of any known or unknown slippages or open doors to avoid becoming lukewarm or undisciplined. If one possesses this hidden quality but does not know how to release it, keep reading.

When it comes down to our *Spiritual Lampstands*, we need to know what we are doing with our senses. In a world filled with distractions, the struggle to keep our minds focused and present can often feel overwhelming. Nevertheless, becoming aware of the gateways through which we experience and interact with the world can help us tame and quiet the wandering mind. In addition, it can also assist with shifting focus, getting in touch with ourselves from the inside out, and becoming attuned to our surroundings.

Our mind tends to roam on its own, especially when we allow the free radicals of life to wander off or roam freely, doing whatever they like. If we do not gain control of our senses, our instincts will be affected, throwing us off-balance from a Spiritual Perspective, even while pretending to have it all together. Unfortunately, this is how the Spiritually Anointed misses the mark with people, places, and things designed to sift, yoke, or soul-tie them. Why is this so important? It is due to the fact that no one is exempt from all of the processes of sight, sound, touch, taste, and smell.

We are all given something to work with, and if we have them all intact and fully functioning, we must become aware of them and use them, *As It Pleases God*. Why are they so important in the Eye of God? The senses in our bodies are designed to inform us or illuminate us through our Spiritual Compass, Conscience, or Instincts. If we are unaware of them, we limit our Spiritual Capacity by default, because this is one of the SECRET and CODED ways that God will speak to us, *Spirit to Spirit*.

If we are not in tune with ourselves, we will miss, misinterpret, or mix up the signals due to some form of Spiritual Blockage.

Although blockages may vary from person to person based on our conditioning, biases, mindset, character, etc., our senses do not vary. We are all blessed with senses; even if not physically due to some form of handicap, we definitely have them Spiritually. More importantly, by not understanding this fact, we as a people miss the Power of Illumination due to our known or unknown self or people-imposed limitations.

Those who are disabled are more apt to depend upon their Spiritual Senses to function from day to day. Although this baffles the minds of those who are not handicapped, it does not change the fact that it is available to all. For this one reason, due to our obliviousness, we will find those who are not suffering from apparent disabilities judging those who have them, and those who have obvious disabilities judging those who appear not to have the obvious. When in all actuality, we all have stunted growth somewhere, with someone, with something, or somehow; yet, we are blessed enough to veil it from the veiled, but not from the Spiritually Unveiled. What does this mean? We can run, but we cannot hide from God. So, we should be exhibiting gratefulness instead of judgment.

When it is all said and done, judgmental biases or demeanor block our Spiritual Light, regardless of how well we play pretend. Now, to ensure we can become Spiritually Illuminated to what cannot be seen, touched, tasted, heard, or smelled on a physical level, we should always exhibit gratefulness, especially for the simple things we take for granted. What do we take for granted? When was the last time we gave thanks for being able to see the beauty life offers, hear the sound of our loved ones, feel the pleasure of having a hug or kiss, taste the goodness of our favorite meal, and smell the aroma that fills the air?

The Power of our Spiritual Adaptation as it relates to our Spiritual Senses has a profound effect on our conscious, subconscious, and unconscious attitudes, thoughts, behaviors, and maneuverability, which has been overlooked, underestimated, devalued, hidden, questioned, and misinterpreted from the beginning of time. What does this mean in layman's terms? We can adapt to our Spiritual Consciousness by regrafting our perception to incorporate what God has in mind for us from His Divine Perspective.

How can we adapt *As It Pleases God*? It is done by stepping into the Spiritual Classroom of Mental, Physical, Emotional, and Spiritual Regrafting. What is this? It is the ability to uproot our worldly conditioning or biases to the Spiritual Dominance of our Divine Birthrights, Promises, Blueprint, or Destiny. Thus, positioning us to take possession of what rightly belongs to us while confidently maximizing our Spiritual Gifts, Creativity, and Talents in their respective places.

The moment we avail ourselves to replace our Spiritual Hardware (the soulish root or governing factors of our thoughts, behaviors, attitude, perception, etc.), we avail ourselves to exhibit the Spiritual Software (the conscious output of Love, Joy, Peace, Patience, Kindness, Goodness, Faithfulness, Gentleness, and Self-Control). Regardless of whether we use the Fruits of the Spirit as Seeds, Oil, or Ammunition, they are designed to help all things work together for our good, training our soulish man to conform, develop, and correct our conscience before the Holy Spirit does the chastening for us. What does this mean? It is best to self-correct before Spiritual Correction takes place. In my opinion, a soulish beatdown is more grueling than a physical one!

When it comes down to the conscious or unconscious Realm of the Spirit, we can opt for the scientific or the unverified way if we like, but the bottom line is that God does not change, whereas we do. Plus, our experiences are unique, giving us or playing back our inner phenomena, be it in the light or darkness, the show will go on to build or take down. So, we cannot become lukewarm in this process or opt for worldly perspectives of deception, tearing down the human psyche without having Spiritual Truths or Integrity backing it up. What does this mean? The 'just because' takedown is a Spiritual Violation.

We cannot call out or pinpoint the negative, unfruitful, or evil and leave it hanging as a dangling modifier to hurt, harm, or traumatize someone, as if we are not doing any wrong in the Eye of God. We must fill in the gap with positive fruits, encouragement, mentoring, or a solution, *As It Pleases God*. Does it really make a difference? Absolutely! Our Spiritual Fruits are the result of the Holy Spirit's work. Without them, it is evidence of the absence of Him and the presence of underlying flawed qualities, displeasing to God.

For example, someone said to me that if they knew their girlfriend was going to leave them for another man, they would have gotten her pregnant before she left. I thought this was appalling. This selfish 'just because' takedown of someone without any form of repentance blocks the Spiritual Healing of his loss, causing suppression of the feelings of being duped.

I advised, 'To impregnate someone without their consent on purpose to keep them is outright evil.' So, as a concerned friend, I kindly helped him pinpoint the root of the matter, assuming total responsibility for his role and point of misdirection. In addition, I also stated, 'If he changed the way he was speaking negativity over his life to a more positive way of doing so, his relational issues with women would be half-solved. By doing so, this would allow him to heal before taking this same issue into the next relationship.'

When selfishly, begrudgingly, or negatively changing the trajectory of someone's life, especially the innocent, to satiate inner insecurities or alleviate stress, it has serious Spiritual Implications, regardless of how we attempt to justify our behavior. Why is this such a big deal in the Eye of God? It is a violation of free will; therefore, we must tread with caution in this matter to avoid getting our *Spiritual Lampstand* snatched away.

We must examine ourselves and our motives often to avoid cross-contaminating our genuineness with worldliness, jealousy, envy, pride, greed, covetousness, hatefulness, and waywardness, appearing Spiritual. Why does God frown on us when faking Spirituality as Believers? It confuses or deceives the innocent, turning them away from Him and the Kingdom altogether.

We are designed to cross-pollinate with the Good News, the Fruits of the Spirit, and Christlike Character, building the Kingdom, not tearing it down. Our undeveloped or untrained Spirituality, *As It Pleases God*, will cause us to search for God in a relationship with others. Most often, we do not understand that we must establish a *Spirit to Spirit* Relationship with our Heavenly Father to better relate to ourselves, spreading outwardly to others.

Once we take ownership of our *Spiritual Lampstand*, we are called to help enlighten the path of another. How? By taking them by the hand, leading them on a journey to Spiritual Awakening. If we digress in this formality, bringing darkness, we are accountable, period.

As a Spiritual Vessel, we have a responsibility to the Kingdom of Heaven; we cannot show up when we feel like it. As *"God is our refuge and strength, a very present help in trouble."* Psalm 46:1. He uses people like us to accomplish His great works; therefore, when He calls upon us, the 'hold on a minute' mentality will not work. We need to have a 'here am I' mentality to keep our light shining brightly.

Why do we need to become open to God? First, He is the Creator of all things. Secondly, outside of God, no one's perspective is absolute! We are all different; this is why we have different fingerprints, footprints, and eyeprints as a Divine Reminder. The moment we think we are above God, having all the answers, not needing Him at all, He will flip the switch on us, bringing us back down to reality from the inside out. For this reason, we must remain humble, allowing Divine Knowledge, Wisdom, Understanding, and Know-How to flow to and through us. If it stops with us, we become unusable in the Kingdom.

We must remain Spiritually Sharp, using God's Word as Kingdom Leverage. Here is what Hebrews 4:12 has to say about this: *"For the word of God is living and powerful, and sharper than any two-edged sword, piercing even to the division of soul and spirit, and of joints and marrow, and is a discerner of the thoughts and intents of the heart."* If we omit using it when we have every opportunity to do so, God will allow the enemy to have a field day with our Mind, Body, and Soul, causing Spiritual Oppression.

What type of God would allow us to become Spiritually Oppressed? The ONE that LOVES us. Here is the first reason from Hebrews 12:6: *"For whom the LORD loves He chastens, and scourges every son whom He receives."* Secondly, it prevents us from becoming Spiritually Dull, according to Ecclesiastes 10:10: *"If the ax is dull, and one does not sharpen the edge, then he must use more strength; but wisdom brings success."*

Our sharpness is being used as a Spiritual Tool to reap or take possession of our Spiritual Birthrights, Promises, and Blessings if we align ourselves properly. Really? Yes, really! To ensure that we are crystal clear on this one, here is what Isaiah 49:2-4 says: *"And He has made my mouth like a sharp sword; in the shadow of His hand He has hidden me, and made me a polished shaft; in His quiver He has hidden me. And He said to me, You are My servant, O Israel, In whom I will be glorified. Then I said, I have labored in vain, I have spent my strength for nothing and in vain; yet surely my just reward is with the LORD, and my work with my God."*

As we are all a work-in-progress, we cannot stop short when it comes down to our *Spiritual Lampstand* or Sharpness. According to the Heavenly of Heavens, it prepares the way for such a time as this. Listed below are a few Revelatory Declarations:

- ☐ *"And to the angel of the church in Pergamos write, These things says He who has the sharp two-edged sword: I know your works, and where you dwell, where Satan's throne is. And you hold fast to My name, and did not deny My faith even in the days in which Antipas was My faithful martyr, who was killed among you, where Satan dwells. But I have a few things against you, because you have there those who hold the doctrine of Balaam, who taught Balak to put a stumbling block before the children of Israel, to eat things sacrificed to idols, and to commit sexual immorality. Thus you also have those who hold the doctrine of the Nicolaitans, which thing I hate. Repent, or else I will come to you quickly and will fight against them with the sword of My mouth."* Revelation 2:12-16.

- ☐ *"Here is the patience of the saints; here are those who keep the commandments of God and the faith of Jesus. Then I heard a voice from heaven saying to me, Write: Blessed are the dead who die in the Lord from now on. Yes, says the Spirit, that they may rest from their labors,* and their works follow them. Then I looked, and behold, a white cloud, and on the cloud sat One like the Son of Man, having on His head a golden crown, and in His hand a sharp sickle." Revelation 14:12-14.

- [ ] "And another angel came out of the temple, crying with a loud voice to Him who sat on the cloud, Thrust in Your sickle and reap, for the time has come for You to reap, for the harvest of the earth is ripe." Revelation 14:15.

- [ ] "So He who sat on the cloud thrust in His sickle on the earth, and the earth was reaped. Then another angel came out of the temple which is in heaven, he also having a sharp sickle." Revelation 14:16-17.

- [ ] "And another angel came out from the altar, who had power over fire, and he cried with a loud cry to him who had the sharp sickle, saying, Thrust in your sharp sickle and gather the clusters of the vine of the earth, for her grapes are fully ripe." Revelation 14:18.

- [ ] "So the angel thrust his sickle into the earth and gathered the vine of the earth, and threw it into the great winepress of the wrath of God." Revelation 14:19.

- [ ] "And the winepress was trampled outside the city, and blood came out of the winepress, up to the horses' bridles, for one thousand six hundred furlongs." Revelation 14:20.

According to the Heavenly of Heavens, our *Spiritual Lampstand* is on the line. We have been lured away from our faith with the superficialities of God's method of operation by running around doing our own thing, pleasing ourselves. But more importantly, before we move on, let me interject scripture to align what I am sharing, "*Now to him that is of power to establish you according to my gospel, and the preaching of Jesus Christ, according to the revelation of the mystery,* which was kept secret since the world began, But now is made manifest, and by the scriptures of the prophets, according to the commandment of the everlasting God, made known to all nations for the obedience of faith: To God only wise, be glory through Jesus Christ forever. Amen." Romans 16:25-27.

Why is our faith so important? It is because *"For in the righteousness of God is revealed from faith to faith, as it is written, the just shall live by faith."* Romans 1:17. It does not say, *"The just shall live by doubt, confusion, hate, and negativity."* If we decide to live in this manner, as it relates to our *Spiritual Lampstand*, it leads to unrighteous living, behaving, thinking, speaking, etc.; therefore, we must make corrections immediately. Self-correcting ensures it does not manifest or snowball into outright rebellion from the inside out while dealing with the Wrath of God. How is this possible when we have the free will to do, say, and become whatever we desire? Amid our choices, if we lie to God, ourselves, and others, deception is inevitable, creating Spiritual Violations in the Kingdom. Instead of remaining free, we place ourselves in bondage without realizing we are doing so due to our lack of Spiritual Understanding or Revelation.

Now, before we move on, to be in the '*Spiritual Know*,' we must understand this: *"For the wrath of God is revealed from heaven against all ungodliness and unrighteousness of men, who hold the truth in unrighteousness; because that which may be known of God is manifest in them; for God hath shown unto them. For the invisible things of him from the creation of the world are clearly seen, being understood by the things that are made, even His eternal power and Godhead; so that they are without excuse: Because that, when they knew God, they glorified Him not as God, neither were thankful; but became vain in their imaginations, and their foolish heart was darkened. Professing themselves to be wise, they became fools, and changed the glory of the uncorruptible God into an image made like to corruptible man, and to birds, and four-footed beasts, and creeping things. Wherefore God also gave them up to uncleanness through the lusts of their own hearts, to dishonor their own bodies between themselves: Who changed the truth of God into a lie, and worshipped and served the creature more than the Creator, who is blessed forever. Amen."* Romans 1:18-25.

What makes this information so important to us? In such a time as this, we are looking for the End-Time Prophecies from the outside, thinking that the Revelation of God will send outer abominations that we can see with our physical eyes. Meanwhile, the Battle of Armageddon is WITHIN the human psyche (the soul of man), and if we keep looking for the outer illusional conditions of what is to come, we will miss the inner aspects of what is already.

For the first time in history, we can openly meme or loom curses over Presiding Authorities and get away with it! Where is the RESPECT? Due to our Spiritual Blindness, Deafness, and Muteness, we openly curse ourselves, our Bloodline, or our Destiny, and we cannot see the implications of doing so.

From my perspective, the desire to be politically correct, sugarcoating things to satiate the soul, cannot contend with owning up to God's truth. What is the truth? The truth about how we have the power to bless ourselves or bring curses to the forefront of our lives, eventually targeting our children.

But more importantly, for the sake of our generational *Spiritual Lampstand*, let me take this to scripture, *"Therefore thou art inexcusable, O man, whosoever thou art that judgest: for wherein thou judgest another, thou condemnest thyself; for thou that judgest doest the same things. But we are sure that the judgment of God is according to truth against them which commit such things. And thinkest thou this, O man, that judgest them which do such things, and doest the same, that thou shalt escape the judgment of God? Or despisest thou the riches of his goodness and forbearance and longsuffering; not knowing that the goodness of God leadeth thee to repentance? But after thy hardness and impenitent heart treasurest up unto thyself wrath against the day of wrath and revelation of the righteous judgment of God; Who will render to every man according to his deeds: To them who by patient continuance in well doing seek for glory and honor and immortality, eternal life: But unto them that are contentious, and do not obey the truth, but obey unrighteousness, indignation and wrath, Tribulation and anguish, upon every soul of man that doeth evil, of the Jew first, and also of the Gentile; But glory, honor, and peace, to every man that worketh good, to the Jew first, and also to the Gentile: For there is no respect of persons with God. For as many as have sinned without law shall also perish without law: and as many as have sinned in the law shall be judged by the law; For not the hearers of the law [are] just before God, but the doers of the law shall be justified. For when the Gentiles, which have not the law, do by nature the things contained in the law, these, having not the law, are a law unto themselves: Which show the work of the law written in their hearts, their conscience also bearing witness, and their thoughts the mean while accusing or else excusing one another, in the day when God shall judge the secrets of men by Jesus Christ according to my gospel."* Romans 2:1-16.

The Spiritual Hindsight of yesterday and today paves the way for us to become positive, fruitful, proactive, and conducively equipped with Spiritual Insight and Foresight for change, circumventing any biases we have about the Wrath of God or His Divine Favor. The inner traumas we are facing are all written in the Word of God in hindsight, but due to our biases and conditioning, we overlook these truths, hidden in plain sight. Spiritually Speaking, we need all the Spiritual Tools to prepare us to sit at the Table without being led astray by vain devices or distractions.

In or out of what we are faced with, we must not focus all of our attention on practical ways to solve Spiritual Issues. Why must Believers become focused, *As It Pleases God*? It is practical deception that causes Spiritual Issues in the first place. Therefore, we must take a different approach to avoid becoming yoked by the system. Simply put, we must take a look within our system to find the seed or point of origination, bringing a resolve from the inside out, not from the outside in. What is the reason for doing so? We are Spirit first.

Always remember, the Holy Spirit knows more than we do! And, He is able to provide Divine Revelation to the things of the Great Unknown. If we dare to take heed to the Spiritual Seals and cover ourselves with the Blood of Jesus as a formal sacrifice, we can use the Word of God as our Weapon of Warfare to combat the lies or the deception of ourselves and others. Doing so helps build the confidence needed to go to the next level of Spirituality while boldly coming to the *Throne of God* and *As It Pleases Him*.

Chapter 6

THRONE ROOM

When coming to the *Throne Room* of God, we must come ready, willing, and able to do what is needed, *As It Pleases Him*. The *Throne Room* of God is not set in stone, nor is it a place to play games or mock His Presence. It is a place to engage Spirit to Spirit with our Heavenly Father to download, upload, or reload information, instructions, decrees, know-how, how-to, or whatever is needed to facilitate our Heaven on Earth experience in Earthen Vessels.

As I spoke earlier about the Mind, Body, Soul, and Spirit, it is for our use in the *Throne Room* where we must rightly divide the Mind and Soul. What is the purpose of doing so? Just so we are crystal clear, let me take it to scripture, *"For this is the covenant that I will make with the house of Israel after those days, says the LORD: I will put My laws in their mind and write them on their hearts; and I will be their God, and they shall be My people. None of them shall teach his neighbor, and none his brother, saying, 'Know the LORD,' for all shall know Me, from the least of them to the greatest of them."* Hebrews 8:10-11.

Spiritual Consistency is needed to establish our Earthly Sanctuary or *Throne Room* to ensure we can live by example through the Fruits of the Spirit, Christlike Character, and the Blood of Jesus as our sacrifice of Spiritual Atonement. Really? Yes, really. Biblically, it says, *"So Christ was offered once to bear the sins of many. To those who eagerly wait for Him He will appear a second time, apart from sin, for salvation."* Hebrews 9:28.

In and out of our daily living, we often hear about a *Throne Room*, Earthly Sanctuary, or the Throne of God; yet, we fail to understand its importance in the Kingdom of Heaven as it relates to our Earthen Vessel. What is the importance of what we are overlooking? According to scripture, it says: *"Let us therefore come boldly to the throne of grace, that we may obtain mercy and find grace to help in time of need."* Hebrews 4:16. Bottom line, we all need help and mercy from our Heavenly Father, regardless of how self-sufficient we have become.

The Throne or Seat in Heaven is designed for us and through us, giving us the ability to operate according to the Will of God while we are still trapped in time. How is this possible? For all things Spiritual, it is a matter of sectioning out a place and time of worship, devotion, and reverence, Mentally, Physically, Emotionally, and Spiritually. If we do not have time or a place for God, ourselves, and others, our *Spirit to Spirit* Relationship cannot be fully consummated.

Is consummation just for married couples? Spiritually, this is where we are deceived. Consummation is used as completeness, wholeness, or fullness in the Realm of the Spirit.

Contrary to what most would think, we are married to our Heavenly Father, ourselves, our family, etc.; if not, division takes place, and unrighteousness will prevail. Blasphemy, right? Wrong. *"For your Maker is your husband, the Lord of host is His name; and your Redeemer is the Holy One of Israel; He is called the God of the whole earth."* Isaiah 54:5.

Spiritually, this type of marriage means joined together in Oneness in a *Spirit to Spirit* (I AM) Relationship. In this type of Spiritual Union, the Biblical Truths of Love have no gender biases. Why? The Spirit of God is Absolute. If we get caught up in gender, we will miss the Divine Message. Now, just so we are crystal clear, let us take it to scripture, *"Let us be glad and rejoice and give Him glory, for the marriage of the Lamb has come, and His wife has made herself ready. And to her it was granted to be arrayed in fine linen, clean and bright, for the fine linen is the righteous acts of the saints. Then he said to me, Write: 'Blessed are those who are called to the marriage supper of the Lamb! And he said to me, these are the true sayings of God."* Revelation 19:7-9.

How is it possible to marry our children? We have a covenant relationship with our offspring, regardless of whether we live up to the agreement or not. What is the Spiritual Covenant that bonds the parent-child relationship? *"Train up a child in the way he should go, and when he is old, he will not depart from it."* Proverbs 22:6. With this live-wired covenant, we have the choice of making it worldly or Godly. Whatever we decide, it will bear the fruits of our labor, so we must exercise extreme caution. In my opinion, this is why we need to become intimately connected to the Throne of God, *As It Pleases Him.*

Due to the lack of understanding regarding Spiritual Marriages, Covenants, and Truths, brokenness is running rampant among Believers, who find themselves bonded to the enemy Mentally, Physically, Emotionally, or Spiritually. When our souls are traumatized, yoked, sifted, or broken, it affects the relational aspects of our Divine Design.

For example, if our Spirit lays dormant, we cannot engage in a relationship of Oneness with God, ourselves, our husband, wife, children, etc. Our Spirit must be Spiritually Awakened to better understand the things of the Spirit. If not, division, selfishness, jealousy, envy, coveting, greed, ulterior motives, control, etc., creep in to sift us. It will also place us on a Mental or Emotional rollercoaster, affecting our Physical aspects of living in due time. What is the purpose of this? It is all due to our lack of Spiritual Understanding, Protocol, and Throne Privileges.

For me, the Throne means *'Through One.'* Through One Sovereignty. Through One God. Through One Authority. Through One I AM. Through One Mission. Through One Relationship. If we can regraft our MINDSET into Spiritual Oneness, *As It Pleases God,* He will *'Unveil the Veiled.'* How do I know? *"After these things I looked, and behold, a door standing open in Heaven. And the first voice which I heard as like a trumpet speaking with me, saying, Come up here, and I will show you things which must take place after this."* Revelation 4:1.

How can we develop this sort of Divine Mindset for the *Throne Room*? It takes time to develop a *Spirit to Spirit* Relationship with God because we must learn and understand His Divine Language, *As It Pleases Him*. However, listed below are a few things we need to know, but not limited to such:

- ☐ We must prepare ourselves to take a seat, relax, and focus in our *Throne Room*.
- ☐ We must enter our *Throne Room* like a stone (state of seriousness) without distractions.
- ☐ We must enter our *Throne Room* happy and vibrant.
- ☐ We must adequately adorn or set up our *Throne Room* appropriately.
- ☐ We must adequately dress ourselves before entering our *Throne Room*.
- ☐ We must enter our *Throne Room* with an expectation to hear from the Heavenly of Heavens.
- ☐ We must remove doubtfulness; doubt gets us booted out of the frequency!
- ☐ We must prepare ourselves to receive Divine Illumination in our *Throne Room*.

As I stated earlier, *Kingdom Transparency* is required for our undisputed Heavenly Experience, *As It Pleases God*. Most often, we are looking for the answers from the Book of Revelation of things to come, when it is all about 'REVEALING' ourselves to ourselves for the purging process.

With all due respect, we bring in Theologians to complicate Spiritual Simplicities regarding the Keys to the Kingdom or the Secrets of the Great Unknown, making people afraid or unworthy of the truth. Yes, the truth about God, themselves, and others. In all reality, the Holy Spirit will teach us everything we need to know according to our Predestined Blueprint.

For example, when entering the Presence of my Heavenly Father, I come humbly knowing nothing, and He grants me Divine

Wisdom beyond human reasoning. I come in with a clean slate to glean for the Kingdom like a pen of a ready writer with the Fruits of the Spirit chiseled into my heart with Christlike Character. More importantly, the same Holy Spirit that feeds me this information will feed anyone who Spiritually Aligns themselves, *As It Pleases God*, with clean hands and a pure heart.

Listen, in the presence of the Holy of Holies, there is nothing hidden. Spiritually Speaking, this has become the biggest Spiritual Cover-up known to man. Now, if we hide from ourselves, we can become unusable in this phase.

When we deceive ourselves or play pretend, we will subconsciously or unconsciously think that we can slip through the cracks with trickery or without repentance. From a Spiritual Perspective, this is perceived as a Deceptive Spirit, which will prevent us from worshiping as we should or possessing our Spiritual Birthrights or Blueprint.

Just so we are clear, we do not have to be perfect to enter our *Throne Room* of Grace; we simply need to be honest, faithful, grateful, and worthy of our Spiritual Crown to be able to read the Secret Seals. What does all of this mean? Let us take it to scripture, *"And I saw in the right hand of Him who sat on the throne a scroll written inside and on the back, sealed with seven seals. Then I saw a strong angel proclaiming with a loud voice, 'Who is worthy to open the scroll and to loose its seals?' And no one in Heaven or on the earth or under the earth was able to open the scroll, or to look at it. So I wept much, because no one was found worthy to open and read the scroll, or to look at it. But one of the elders said to me, 'Do not weep. Behold, the Lion of the tribe of Judah, the Root of David, has prevailed to open the scroll and to loose its seven seals.' And I looked, and behold, in the midst of the throne and of the four living creatures, and in the midst of the elders, stood a Lamb as though it had been slain, having seven horns and seven eyes, which are the seven Spirits of God sent out into all the earth. Then He came and took the scroll out of the right hand of Him who sat on the throne."* Revelation 5:1-7. What does this mean for Believers? All hope is not lost.

If one follows my lead, one would be worthy enough to read the Spiritual Scrolls of Heaven. How is this possible? I am a mere

Messenger of the Good News; I do not pull any punches when it comes down to the things of Heaven or its Treasures hidden in plain sight.

What makes the Spiritual Seals so important? If we do not take the time to understand the time in which we are living, we will build a bed that is set up for our own extermination. How is this possible? If we take a moment to look at the word Seals, it means closure. But, if we look even closer, from my perspective, the word Seals reads in reverse; it says slaes (slays), which means annihilation or massacre. Whereas from a human perspective, we would view this as a physical occurrence, such as with a weapon of mass destruction, but it is not! What does this mean? All of this will take place from within the inner psyche of man (the soul).

If we self-destruct, who is to blame? We are, right? But more importantly, if we do this to ourselves, then there is no Spiritual Recompense needed. The enemy gets away scot-free. We cannot blame anyone for what we do or bring upon ourselves from the inside out due to our free will. They are only accountable for the outside approach or seed planted through manipulation, bullying, and lying, which has a lesser offense (a slap on the hand) than taking the life of another or shedding innocent blood. Is this fair? Of course, it is fair.

We have the choice of watering a seed or uprooting it, period. If we take a seed and run with it, bearing fruit, we cannot blame another. We must take responsibility for the seed, whether it is good, bad, or indifferent. Therefore, we must be cautious about becoming a victim of such atrocities. Let us take this a step further from a Spiritual Perspective. The Seals of the 'Come and See' or the 'Big Reveal' are comprised of:

- ☐ The Seal of Religious Deception. *Revelation 6:1-2.*
- ☐ The Seal of Conflict. *Revelation 6:3-4.*
- ☐ The Seal of Scarcity. *Revelation 6:5-6.*
- ☐ The Seal of Death. *Revelation 6:7-8.*
- ☐ The Seal of Martyrdom of the Church. *Revelation 6:9-11.*
- ☐ The Seal of Planetary Imbalances. *Revelation 6:12-17.*

☐ The Seal of Heavenly Silence. *Revelation 8:1-6.*

All of these Seals are signs of the time we are in right now; however, it does not determine our place in the Kingdom unless we choose to develop a deaf ear, become paralyzed with fear, or willfully take part in becoming and remaining a victim.

How can we not become a victim when we are surrounded by death and destruction? Always remember, the fight is already fixed for Spiritual Victory. Most will look for this Victory from outside circumstances and conditions, but our Spiritual Victory is from within. Our faith, mindset, and perception, used with our Fruits of the Spirit and Christlike Character, are our means of preparation. Spiritually, this will keep us a step ahead when others are walking around thinking that hatefulness, cruelty, and evil practices are going to keep them on top of their game.

If the enemy divides us from the inside out, we can become easily defeated. If the enemy can keep us stuck on the negative, we will not have the power to withstand the wiles of the enemy because we are too busy secretly fighting against ourselves. If we do not build strength from within, soon enough, we will begin to fight against each other, breaking the foundation of our homes first, then spreading outwardly, thinking we are right in our own eyes. How is this possible? Suppose we are Spiritually Blind, Deaf, or Mute. In this case, it means that we are Spiritually Veiled from knowing and understanding certain things about ourselves and what is taking place around us, resulting in feelings of hopelessness and lack of Spiritual Purpose, Placement, or Belonging.

In or out of Kingdom Principles, if we have a desire to remain in the dark, feeling an inner void, then so be it; we have free will to do so. However, we are called to be in the Light, or better yet, the 'Spiritual Know,' closing the Spiritual Gap on any form of known or unknown void. With the Spiritual Fullness Therein, it gives us the ability to get to the root of matters without having the surface hoopla to shift us negatively. Thus, we are able to ask the right questions or receive the correct answers before judging what we do not understand.

Everyone and everything has a story. Getting an understanding helps us to reflect on God's Grace and Mercy, shifting our perspective to create a win-win by looking for the good or creating some form of opportunity.

Suppose we miss the mark on creating rational approaches to life. In this case, we will subject ourselves to the irrational elements designed to sift us Mentally, Physically, Emotionally, and Spiritually, causing us to become a part of the Spiritual Seals as opposed to being able to read them. When we are moved by selfishness, jealousy, pride, greed, coveting, competitiveness, and pompousness, we will not see what we are supposed to see from a Spiritual Perspective.

For example, when someone gets angry, they may feel justified in cursing someone out, even if it is not their fault. Do we think for a minute the person partaking in this negative behavior cares about someone's feelings? Apparently not, because this unwarranted behavior in the Kingdom is a big no-no. Even Moses was denied the ability to go into the Promised Land due to his uncontrollable anger and lack of self-control. Although we are not Moses, the same Spiritual Principles apply to us in today's day and age. When it comes down to God's sheep, He has zero tolerance for crushing the innocent or for conscious immorality, period.

We can sit around kiking (gossiping) it up, thinking we are getting away with our folly, but unfortunately, it does not become lost in the Spiritual Scrolls. Unbeknown to most, our Spiritual Scrolls are scripts (observational learning) that will play themselves back when we least expect it, positively or negatively. Really? Yes, really!

If one has children, do we not see ourselves in them? Of course, we do; even if we are in denial, they observe more than we think. Yet, if the script happens to be positive, good, and fruitful, we are quick to take the credit; however, if it is negative, bad, or unfruitful, we are quick to point the finger without analyzing the finger of origination (the root).

Let us take this one step further. If we play violent thoughts in our minds continuously, eventually the violence will make its way to reality when we least expect it in our actions, reactions, attitudes, or our daily lives. So, we definitely want to keep the images in our mind, positive, non-violent, and fruitful to prevent an unwanted outcome or replay. We definitely want our attitudinal character to match our behavior. By doing so, it helps to prevent unwanted pressure to remember our roles or when we are bouncing from one character to another. Is this real? Of course, this is real, especially when we are living a lie or playing pretend!

How can we change our Spiritual Scrolls to reflect a more pleasing and consistent script? Listed below are a few tips, but not limited to such:

- ☐ We must determine what we are targeting, such as behaviors, thoughts, reactions, words, conditioning, attitude, character, etc.
- ☐ We must find the point of origination (the root). Be it explicit (conscious, realized, or obvious) or implicit (unconscious, unrealized, blocked, or hidden) memory. This is a need-to-know.
- ☐ We must understand the 'Why.'
- ☐ We must refuse to take whatever our 'Why' is out on another or point the finger. This is an anti-vendetta or anti-aggression zone.
- ☐ We must repent of any known or unknown hurt, pain, or trauma it may have caused.
- ☐ We must understand the lessons we need to learn.
- ☐ We must decide on the changes that need to be made.
- ☐ We must come up with positive affirmations or scriptures to counteract the temptations.
- ☐ We must understand and document what or who triggers our feelings, responses, emotions, thoughts, behaviors, etc., positively or negatively.
- ☐ We must find a way to create an opportunity or a win-win.

- ☐ We must target the Fruits of the Spirit that are associated with our challenge and maximize them accordingly.
- ☐ We must be willing to help, mentor, and leave breadcrumbs or a trail of wisdom for another.

In or out of our *Throne Room*, we must make a willing attempt to change for the better, superseding the worldly system of operation. If we choose to remain the same, doing our own thing, we will become limited as it relates to Kingdom Principles. We are required to grow! Without growth, we become stunted by default, preventing us from taking full advantage of the Spiritual Principles designed to take us to the next level, *As It Pleases God*.

Spiritual Deviation causes Mental, Physical, Emotional, and Spiritual Deprivation. Why would we become Spiritually Deprived? First and foremost, we are Spirit. If we knowingly or unknowingly starve ourselves Spiritually, we will have a hunger from within by Divine Default, resulting in thirsty thoughts, emotions, behaviors, and the list goes on. Even if we condition ourselves to cover it up with positive affirmations, it still can be heard through our actions, reactions, words, or perception, making us wishy-washy, inconsistent, or, as the Bible calls it, lukewarm.

According to scripture, it says, *"I know your works, that you are neither cold nor hot. I could wish you were cold or hot. So then, because you are lukewarm, and neither cold nor hot, I will vomit you out of My mouth."* Revelation 3:15-16. Why is this the case when we are not perfect? The goal is to become true to ourselves, and if we are walking around faking it, this is where God has an issue with us.

For example, we have someone who speaks great things in front of others, pleading the Blood of Jesus all over the place. Still, behind closed doors, they speak to a family member like a junkyard dog, looming curses all over their family members (their Bloodline) without any form of reservation. What a contradiction, right? Absolutely. We may take this sort of behavior for granted, but God does not. He considers our deeds and heart posture to determine whether we are lukewarm. Listed below are a few instances of lukewarmness, but not limited to such:

- ☐ When we use God for the benefit without giving a second thought about being in Purpose on purpose, this is lukewarm behavior.
- ☐ When we find ourselves always begging for help from God, without helping ourselves or others, this is lukewarm behavior.
- ☐ When we use the Bible to justify our behavior or whitewash scripture without repenting, correcting, or changing, this is lukewarm behavior.
- ☐ When we pretend to obey God, and we secretly exhibit rebellion by not listening or disrespecting others, especially our elders, this is lukewarm behavior.
- ☐ When we are unwilling to help others, even if it is within our power to do so, this is lukewarm behavior.
- ☐ When we openly or secretly compromise our integrity without any form of remorse, this is lukewarm behavior.
- ☐ When we create known or unknown idols in our lives, putting God on the back burner, this is lukewarm behavior.
- ☐ When we refuse to become transparent and share the Good News, this is lukewarm behavior.
- ☐ When God blesses us and we become selfish, refusing to be a blessing to others, this is lukewarm behavior.
- ☐ When we refuse to exhibit the Fruits of the Spirit or Christlike Character, this is lukewarm behavior.

- ☐ When we look down on others, degrade, crush, turn up our noses, or pass judgment to make ourselves appear better or more blessed than someone else, this is lukewarm behavior.

- ☐ When we become jealous, envious, covetous, greedy, hateful, or wayward, this is lukewarm behavior.

The clash of good and evil is in the power of our words, thoughts, behaviors, and decisions. Contrary to what we are conditioned to believe, they are inadvertently designed to convey the beliefs or biases residing in the contents of our hearts, regardless of whether we desire them to become known or not. When placed under the right conditions, pushed to the limit, or faced with a certain trauma, the contents of our hearts will come forth. Spiritually, this is why God will break, train, yoke, and test us before commissioning.

Now, if we commission ourselves without stepping into the Spiritual Classroom, then this is another reason why we get the lukewarm individuals pretending to be Heaven-Sent. As a result, with all due respect, we have a saturation of false prophets misleading the innocent with worldly doctrine appearing Spiritual, without any form of healing from the inside out or Spiritual Revelation.

Although the credibility of the church is under fire, the Mission of God is not. All the hoopla is designed to create doubt and hopelessness in those who have underlying hurts, traumas, or strongholds, causing them to want to give up. Once we give up on ourselves, we will fall for anything or anyone, causing a great derailment of our Divine Destiny.

Although the enemy can steal, glean, or zap our power, sifting us negatively or outright yoking us to the core. Yet, they cannot steal our Divine Destiny, Promises, or Birthrights unless we willfully give them up. For this reason, we cannot lose hope, no matter what.

As long as we have breath in our bodies, we will always have a ray of hope because change is inevitable. The Cycle of Life is on our side; as long as the sun rises and sets daily, our SEASON will come if we stay focused, faithful, and consistent. If we do not know this information, we will give it all up to make the pain, trauma, yoke, or whatever go away, not realizing it is only temporary.

What is more, if we do not realize what the fight is all about, we will shy away from capitalizing on our Gifts, Talents, Creativity, or Calling as we should.

So, here is the deal: we must begin to pay attention to God, ourselves, others, and life. They are all trying to relay a message, and we do not want to miss it. Plus, if we can redirect our Mission to one of healing, motivation, mentoring, building, and encouragement, we can defeat the enemy. How is this possible? Once we are healed Mentally, Physically, and Emotionally, we will Spiritually recognize the Power of God with a desire to share our story, which brings forth our Testament.

In becoming like-minded with our Heavenly Father and creating a *Spirit to Spirit* Relationship with Him, our story is our ministry designed to minister to the life of another. Our Testaments (our lives) will become similar to those of the individuals who shared their Testaments in the Bible that we are using for such a time as this. Really? Yes, really!

According to Revelation 1:19, it says: *"Write the things which you have seen, and the things which are, and the things which will take place after this."* How is it possible to write what we see if we are not articulate? Moses had a stutter, but it did not stop him from doing what He was called to do. So, I say once again, everyone has a story to tell, full of strengths, weaknesses, blessings, tests, lessons, and the list goes on. However, most do not take the time to capture it on paper, causing the enemy to steal our Spiritual Seeds of Legacy due to hidden insecurities. Listen, if I had allowed my apparent disabilities to stop me, you would not be reading this book to partake of 'The Great Reveal.'

Our Gifts, Talents, Creativity, and Calling will most often be hidden in some form of disability, weakness, setback, trauma, or failure. In a world that often glorifies success, prestige, and perfection, it is easy to overlook the profound truths hidden within our struggles, within our insurmountable obstacles, and within our idiosyncrasies. If we do not grow and learn from them, we will hinder ourselves by default. On our Spiritual Journey or pathway to healing on any level, we should not leave any stone unturned. Why not? Most often, it is where our Cornerstone of Greatness and Divine Wisdom are hidden or buried.

Suppose God has laid our Divine Destiny in a disability, setback, weakness, trauma, or failure. In this case, He will provide an Aaron to assist, a ram in the bush, a Shepherd to protect, or a Spiritual Teacher to guide. All of which are based on The-Lord-Will-Provide Spiritual Covenant. In our *Throne Room*, all we need to do is lay claim to it, *As It Pleases God*, from Genesis 22:14: "*So Abraham called the name of the place, The-Lord-Will-Provide; as it is said to this day, 'In the Mount of the Lord it shall be provided.'*"

In or out of the Spiritual Folds of life, we must remove our Spiritual Blinders to see, open our Spiritual Ears to hear, and set a Spiritual Guard over our tongues to know when to speak and when to plead the 5th. What is the need for all of this? Our Testimony should outlive us, mentoring generations to come while revealing our Revelation in two ways:

- ☐ Through *Basic Research* of self to understand our hidden truths, Mentally, Physically, Emotionally, and Spiritually, from our Perspective.

- ☐ Through *Applied Research*, aligning our lives with Biblical Principles, Laws, Precepts, and Concepts, revealing our Gifts, Talents, Creativity, or Calling from God's Divine Perspective, *As It Pleases Him*.

When challenging ourselves to ask fact-finding questions for our Basic or Applied Research, we must document. If we are clueless about our querying process, then ask questions in the *What, When, Where, How, Why,* and with *Whom* form. It can provoke our soul to unveil hidden seeds of Spiritual Deflection, Reflection, or

Measurement, while documenting what we are saying to ourselves and what God has to say.

Furthermore, if captured on paper, it is easier to document God's Divine Counteraction, Revelation, or Correction to what we are feeling, saying, thinking, becoming, or doing. But more importantly, it helps determine Godliness or Ungodliness, righteousness or unrighteousness, positivity or negativity, and the list goes on.

If we attempt to hide all of this in our heads, it will create overloads, breakdowns, confusion, or a lack of clarity. In layman's terms, our inner chatterbox will not know when to be quiet, listen, understand, interpret, absorb, or cast down. Instead, it becomes like a sponge, soaking up everything, causing us to become inconsistent, overwhelmed, or a seemingly unfiltered know-it-all.

As a part of our *'Great Reveal,'* our Testament should never match another man's Testament. We are all unique with different perceptions, conditioning, traumas, and experiences; however, the only aspect that will not change is the Word of God in the aligning or correction process. Now, to avoid inconsistencies in this process, we need to involve the Holy Trinity in governing our human inclinations.

Spiritually Speaking, if we are breathing the Breath of Life, there is no such thing as we have arrived. With Spiritual Elevation, as long as we are living, we all have work to do! Is this Biblical? *"And I fell at his feet to worship him, but he said to me, see that you do not do that! I am your fellow servant, and of your brethren who have the testimony of Jesus. Worship God! For the testimony of Jesus is the Spirit of Prophecy. Now I saw Heaven opened, and behold, a white horse. And He who sat on him was called Faithful and True, and in righteousness He judges and makes war."* Revelation 19:10-11.

The bottom line is that worshiping God takes work, and capturing our Testimony requires more. Why are Believers required to do more? First, we are not properly acclimated to document our Testament until we are given specific instructions, *As It Pleases God*. Secondly, it takes discipline, determination, and proactiveness to capitalize on our Seeds of Greatness that have fallen to the ground, been stolen, hidden, or are bearing fruit.

What do we need to do, or how do we do our part? According to scripture, it says, *"Therefore we also, since we are surrounded by so great a cloud of witnesses, let us lay aside every weight, and the sin which so easily ensnares us, and let us run with endurance the race that is set before us, looking unto Jesus, the author and finisher of our faith, who for the joy that was set before Him endured the cross, despising the shame, and has sat down at the right hand of the throne of God."* Hebrews 12:1-2.

What do we need to do to Spiritually Unveil ourselves, *As It Pleases God*? First, we need to understand who or what we are dealing with. Secondly, we need to repent of all of our atrocities or hindrances, be they known or unknown. Thirdly, we need to agree with those involved, if need be, because a divided house cannot stand in the Kingdom. Fourthly, ask for revelation as Daniel did. Lastly, give thanks and bless the Kingdom of Heaven. Here is the story according to Daniel 2:19-22: *"So Daniel went in and asked the king to give him time, that he might tell the king the interpretation. Then Daniel went to his house, and made the decision known to Hananiah, Mishael, and Azariah, his companions, that they might seek mercies from the God of heaven concerning this secret, so that Daniel and his companions might not perish with the rest of the wise men of Babylon. Then the secret was revealed to Daniel in a night vision. So Daniel blessed the God of heaven. Daniel answered and said: Blessed be the name of God forever and ever, for wisdom and might are His. And He changes the times and the seasons; He removes kings and raises up kings; He gives wisdom to the wise and knowledge to those who have understanding. He reveals deep and secret things; He knows what is in the darkness, and light dwells with Him."*

So, my question to you is, 'What do you see?' 'What are you not seeing?', or better yet, 'What is your big REVEAL?' The looming questions of today, tomorrow, and forever lie in your ability to remove the veil to see what is right before your very eyes. Why must we see clearly? *The Great Reveal* and the *Heavenly of Heavens* are Now!

Chapter 7

HEAVENLY OF HEAVENS

For such a time as this, some would prefer to run underneath a rock and hide. Unfortunately, life does not work in this manner. We must be present, taking a more in-depth look from within, opening the Kingdom of Heaven's hidden secrets. According to scripture, it says: "*See that you do not refuse Him who speaks. For if they did not escape who refused Him who spoke on earth, much more shall we not escape if we turn away from Him who speaks from heaven, whose voice then shook the earth; but now He has promised, saying, Yet once more I shake not only the earth, but also heaven. Now this, 'Yet once more,' indicates the removal of those things that are being shaken, as of things that are made, that the things which cannot be shaken may remain. Therefore, since we are receiving a Kingdom which cannot be shaken, let us have grace, by which we may serve God acceptably with reverence and godly fear. For our God is a consuming fire.*" Hebrews 12:25-29.

When speaking of fire, we often associate it with the process of burning or a consuming hellfire. If we look a little deeper from a Spiritual Perspective, the Spiritual Fire relating to the *Heavenly of Heavens* is associated with:

- ☐ A Passion from within.
- ☐ A Fervor from within.
- ☐ An Intensity from within.
- ☐ A Vigor from within.
- ☐ An Excitement from within.
- ☐ A Conviction from within.

- ☐ A Stance from within.
- ☐ A Knowing from within.
- ☐ A Decree from within.
- ☐ A Peace from within.
- ☐ A Reverence from within.
- ☐ An Agreement from within.

The Spiritual Sparks of Greatness are already within each and every one of us. Still, we need to know this without doubting or wavering. Why do we need to take a look from within? Our true faith comes from within, exhibited outwardly. How is this possible? According to scripture, *"Now faith is the substance of things hoped for, the evidence of things not seen. For by it the elders obtained a good testimony. By faith we understand that the worlds were framed by the word of God, so that the things which are seen were not made of things which are visible."* Hebrews 11:1-3.

What is the *Heavenly of Heavens?* It is our Heavenly Country, similar to an earthly one. To have a Heavenly Language, as we discussed earlier, we must have a Spiritual Place for it as well. Am I pulling for straws here? Absolutely not! Please allow me to align accordingly: *"These all died in faith, not having received the promises, but having seen them afar off were assured of them, embraced them and confessed that they were strangers and pilgrims on the earth. For those who say such things declare plainly that they seek a homeland. And truly if they had called to mind that country from which they had come out, they would have had opportunity to return. But now they desire a better, that is, a Heavenly Country. Therefore God is not ashamed to be called their God, for He has prepared a CITY for them."* Hebrews 11:13-16.

If something is sealed in the rationality of living life, it means the seal is protecting something, right? And that something is on the inside of the seal, right? If the value were outside the seal, there would be no need for a seal. Once again, here is the scripture, *"And I saw in the right hand of Him who sat on the throne a scroll written inside and on the back, sealed with seven seals."* Revelation 5:1.

Listen, if every living creature has an inner knowing of Divine Reverence without having the ability to read or write, it means we have it as well. Nevertheless, we must take an additional step to unveil what has been veiled from the Garden of Eden. How do we go about doing so? Here are four Spiritual Elements that give us authority to sit at the right hand of God in the *Heavenly of Heavens*.

- ☐ The *First Power* is hidden in the Prayers. *"Now when He had taken the scroll, the four living creatures and the twenty-four elders fell down before the Lamb, each having a harp, and golden bowls full of incense, which are the prayers of the saints."* Revelation 5:8.

- ☐ The *Second Power* is hidden in our songs of praise, deliverance, worthability, and redemption. *"And they sang a new song, saying: You are worthy to take the scroll, And to open its seals; For You were slain, and have redeemed us to God by Your blood Out of every tribe and tongue and people and nation, and have made us kings and priests to our God; and we shall reign on the earth."* Revelation 5:9-10.

- ☐ The *Third Power* is hidden in the Spiritual Reverence to the Blood of Jesus, the sacrificial Lamb of God for our sins. *"Then I looked, and I heard the voice of many angels around the throne, the living creatures, and the elders; and the number of them was ten thousand times ten thousand, and thousands of thousands, saying with a loud voice: Worthy is the Lamb who was slain To receive power and riches and wisdom, And strength and honor and glory and blessing!"* Revelation 5:11-12.

- ☐ The *Fourth Power* is hidden in our AMEN. This profound Revelation of singing worshipable tunes into the *Heavenly of Heavenlies* of agreement and gratefulness brings peace to the soul of man like no other. We cannot go wrong by coming into total agreement with God's Divine Will and Ways. *"And every creature which is in heaven and on the earth and under the earth and such as are in the sea, and all that are in them, I heard saying: 'Blessing and honor and glory and power Be to Him who sits on the throne, and to the Lamb, forever and ever!' Then the four living creatures said, 'Amen!' And the twenty-four elders fell down and worshiped Him who lives forever and ever."* Revelation 5:13-14. Unbeknown to most, this is why the Book of Revelation is riddled with the word *'Amen'* to the highest degree.

Regardless of what we see with our physical eyes, we dwell between two realms, Earth and Heaven. How is this possible? Once again, we are Spirit first, dwelling on Earth with a body containing a MIND and SOUL to relate in UNITY. When dwelling between the two realms, we can choose to confuse ourselves, or we can keep it real simple, similar to the way animals do.

"In the beginning God created the Heavens and Earth." Genesis 1:1. The question we should ask is, 'Why are the Heavens plural?' There are multiple layers to God, Spirituality, and the Elements of the Great Unknown, and our Heaven on Earth experience determines our Revelatory Reveal in the end. Once again, everything we need for this experience is already.

Amid all things, we must position ourselves to COME. Or better yet, ARISE *As It Pleases God*. And then, we must AVAIL ourselves to receive the unveiling of Spiritual Prophecy. Really? Yes, really! According to scripture, it says, *"And the Spirit and the bride say, 'Come!' And let him who hears say, 'Come!' And let him who thirsts come. Whoever desires, let him take the water of life freely."* Revelation 22:17. Be it coming to God or coming to ourselves, it is our reasonable service.

God will not make us want what He offers; we must want it for ourselves while cleaning up the clutter from the inside out. Why must we do a clean sweep from the inside out? If we do not, we will begin to add untruths to the Word of God, lie on Him, pimp Him, or play pretend. As a result of doing so, we may yoke ourselves or create generational curses with or without good intentions. Let us take it to scripture, *"For I testify to everyone who hears the words of the prophecy of this book: If anyone adds to these things, God will add to him the plagues that are written in this book; and if anyone takes away from the words of the book of this prophecy, God shall take away his part from the Book of Life, from the holy city, and from the things which are written in this book."* Revelation 22:18-19.

We often do not realize we are creating our own plagues by the way we think, behave, react, speak, or how we condescend others. How can we possibly curse our own hands as Believers? The contents of the heart and the thoughts we think reveal all, whether we realize it or not, especially when left uncorrected or unrepentant, only to please ourselves.

How do we know if we are doing things contrary to the Word of God? Listed below are a few examples, but not limited to such:

- ☐ If we are destroying as opposed to building the Kingdom, ourselves and others, we may have inner issues in need of regrafting.

- ☐ If we have a bad attitude, anger problems, or lack self-control, we may need to step back into the Spiritual Classroom.

- ☐ If we enjoy or thrive on chaos, confusion, and fighting, we may need to seek the Covering of God regarding this matter.

- ☐ If we are full of hate, unforgiveness, envy, jealousy, coveting, or competitiveness, we may need to take a step back to receive inner rectification.

- ☐ If we are mean, spiteful, judgmental, prejudiced, unkind, or rude, we may need to engage in a checkup from the neck up.

- ☐ If we are constantly negative, demeaning, or full of doom and gloom, we may need to restructure our way of thinking.

- ☐ If we cannot control our tongues, or if it is unruly or disrespectful, we may need to revamp our method of operation.

- ☐ If we wish ill will to others without giving it a second thought, we may need to check our conscience.

- ☐ If we think the worst of others without getting to know them or their story, we may need to check our trustworthiness gauge.

- ☐ If our mind is easily sifted, we may need to set a guard to protect ourselves from the Spiritual Bullies.

- ☐ If we cannot retract, openly correct, become transparent about our misunderstandings, or apologize regarding our point of erring, we may need a better understanding of how Divine Revelation works in the Kingdom.

- ☐ If we allow arrogance to make us secretly or openly pompous, we may need to reexamine the life of Jesus, as well as His method of operation and His approach to people, places, things, and life.

According to the *Heavenly of Heavens*, correction, understanding, and maturity come with Spiritual Levels to train and equip the Spiritual Elites from the inside out. What does this mean? The Spiritual Truths, on one level, can be limited until our Spiritual Veil is lifted or expanded to incorporate the Secrets of Heaven.

Spiritual limits will cause us to challenge our perception of Spirituality against Heavenly Meanings of its original intent. What does this mean? When we lack a complete understanding, we will bend the Word of God to fit our lives or agenda instead of using it for healing, guidance, and correction, *As It Pleases Him*.

How can we miss the mark or become limited, especially when we are Spiritually Anointed to interpret the Word of God? As

Spiritual Beings having a human experience, we will all miss the mark or become limited at some point for training purposes. For this reason, we should always heed 1 Samuel 16:7: *"The Lord said to Samuel, Do not look at his appearance or at the height of his stature, because I have refused him. For the Lord does not see as man sees; for man looks at the outward appearance, but the Lord looks at the heart."*

When it comes down to matters of the heart, no one is exempt from Heavenly Limitations. We must continuously work on ourselves to ensure our motives are pure, righteous, and untainted with worldliness, ensuring we do not become confounded, dumbfounded, or sideswiped by the issues of life.

What makes the *Heavenly of Heavens* so vital to us? From my perspective, if we take a look at the word Heaven, for me, if I read it in reverse, it says Nevaeh (Never). What is the most powerful scripture in the Bible containing this word? *"Let your conduct be without covetousness; be content with such things as you have. For He Himself said, I will NEVER leave you nor forsake you."* Hebrews 13:5. If we take a moment to brand this scripture on the tablet of the heart, it unveils the next scripture, *"So we may boldly say, The Lord is my Helper; I will not fear. What can man do to me?"* Hebrews 13:6.

But more importantly, we must also understand that this Spiritual Declaration has a Spiritual Contingency Clause: *"Remember those who rule over you, who have spoken the word of God to you, whose faith follow, considering the outcome of their conduct. Jesus Christ is the same yesterday, today, and forever. Do not be carried about with various and strange doctrines. For it is good that the heart be established by grace, not with foods which have not profited those who have been occupied with them."* Hebrews 13:7-9.

How do we know if the *Heavenly of Heavens* is on our side? When it is BACKING us Mentally, Physically, Emotionally, and Spiritually. How is this possible? We must have a made-up mind of its intent and avail ourselves to our Predestined Blueprint for the sake of the Kingdom of God. According to scripture, it says, *"Now may the God of peace who brought up our Lord Jesus from the dead, that great*

Shepherd of the sheep, through the blood of the everlasting covenant, make you complete in every good work to do His will, working in you what is well pleasing in His sight, through Jesus Christ, to whom be glory forever and ever. Amen." Hebrews 13:20-21.

Unbeknown to most, it is through the BLOOD covenant that the *Heavenly of Heavens* is provoked and ready to revoke our Spiritual Rights at the drop of a dime. Therefore, we should not play around or judge what we do not understand. Our cluelessness can become our downfall, especially when dealing with something or someone covered by the Blood of Jesus and is in Purpose on purpose and using the Fruits of the Spirit, *As It Pleases God*. Really? Yes, really!

In today's day and age, from a Spiritual Perspective as it relates to the *Heavenly of Heavens*, we do not place much emphasis on our Bloodline Profiles, nor do we take into consideration the associated risks of not knowing. However, in the medical industry, we all know that it is all about the blood, period. They can determine a lot by what is in our blood and what is not. But more importantly, they want to know all about our family's medical history, tying what is in their blood to ours as well. Although it seems unfair to prejudge individuals by Bloodline Profiling, they know the power of Bloodline transfers, even if we are aloof to it.

For our sake and the sake of our loved ones, we must understand the Files of our Blood as well, from a Spiritual Perspective. What we digest or internalize Mentally, Physically, Emotionally, and Spiritually becomes the Bloodline Profile of our tomorrow, mirroring its donor.

Just so we are clear, the mirroring effect does not mean it is an inherited trait. The Bloodline Profile of our superego can be regrafted or changed by us and through us if we have a desire to do so while following the proper Spiritual Protocols, *As It Pleases God*. On behalf of the *Heavenly of Heavens*, negative files in our Bloodline can be discarded as well, but before we can discard them, we must first get an understanding to prevent another negative file of the same kind from reappearing.

The bottom line is that the action form of what we see taking place outwardly regarding our Bloodline Profile is not as limited as most would think. What does this mean? The *Heavenly of Heavens* granted us a Spiritual Aspect of our Bloodline. Is this Biblical? Let me counteract this question with another. Are we not covered by the Blood of Jesus due to an action taken on His behalf? Did Jesus go to the Cross as a sacrificial action for our sins? Of course, He did. The Blood of the Spirit cannot get any more powerful than this, but let me take it to scripture anyway. *"But if we walk in the light, as he is in the light, we have fellowship one with another, and the Blood of Jesus Christ his Son cleanses us from all sin."* 1 John 1:7.

When our positive actions come into Divine Alignment with our Spiritual Desires, *As It Pleases God*, they bring light into our lives. To wash away the dark, harmful, or negative files, attempting to stain our Predestined Blueprint, reputation, or good name. For this reason, it is always WISE to cover the LAMPPOST of our house with the Blood of Jesus, especially if we are Mentally, Physically, Emotionally, and Spiritually disturbed by the Vicissitudes of Life.

But more importantly, what we do with what we are taught for such a time as this has a profound impact on what is to come. In order to *'Unveil the Veiled,'* here is what we need to know, beyond a shadow of a doubt: *"John, to the seven churches which are in Asia: Grace to you and peace from Him who is and who was and who is to come, and from the seven Spirits who are before His throne, and from Jesus Christ, the faithful witness, the firstborn from the dead, and the ruler over the kings of the earth. To Him who loved us and washed us from our sins in His own blood, and has made us kings and priests to His God and Father, to Him be glory and dominion forever and ever. Amen."* Revelation 1:4-6.

If we overlook the Spiritual, it will affect the Physical, Mental, and Emotional aspects of our Bloodline Profile. For this reason, we must find balance, *As It Pleases God*. How is it possible to balance things, especially when they are out of control? First, being out of control is a matter of perception. Secondly, we must add God into the equation of all things, *As It Pleases Him*. Thirdly, we must get an understanding of what creates files from within the human psyche. Listed below are a few examples, but not limited to such:

- ☐ What we experience, good, bad, or indifferent, becomes files.
- ☐ What we say or think inwardly or outwardly, positively or negatively, becomes files.
- ☐ Our disappointments, hiccups, or weaknesses become files.
- ☐ What we do, how we behave, and the way we respond from Christlike to worldly character become files.
- ☐ Our fears, hang-ups, habits, or traumas, provoked or unprovoked, natural or conditioned, become files.
- ☐ Our inner or outer chaos or chatter becomes files.
- ☐ Our ability to love or hate becomes files.
- ☐ Our level of peace, or the lack of it from the inside out, becomes files.
- ☐ Our patience or humility, and the lack of them, become files.
- ☐ Our hope or faith becomes files.
- ☐ Our biases or conditioning become files.
- ☐ Our truth becomes files.

I can go on for days with this list, but I am sure I have made my point on how files become a part of our Spiritual Bloodline, Track record, or Evaluation, determining the fruits we bear. Yet, the most important aspect of our files is that we have the power to determine the type of fruit it bears. Or, according to the *Heavenly of Heavens*, we can regraft it, altering the Spiritual DNA structure regardless of what is set to manifest in our physical DNA. How is this possible? We need to understand a few things regarding the Mind of God and His expectations of us, *As It Pleases Him*:

- ☐ We must own our truth without thinking we are above the law or Him. *Therefore by the deeds of the law no flesh will be justified in His sight, for by the law is the knowledge of sin."* Romans 3:20.

- ☐ We must become obedient, making an honest attempt to do what is right in the Sight of God. *"But now the righteousness of*

God apart from the law is revealed, being witnessed by the Law and the Prophets." Romans 3:21.

- [ ] We must faithfully believe in the Holy Trinity. *"Even the righteousness of God, through faith in Jesus Christ, to all and on all who believe. For there is no difference."* Romans 3:22.

- [ ] We must understand that we are all a work-in-progress, making the process of repentance extremely important. *"For all have sinned and fall short of the glory of God."* Romans 3:23.

- [ ] We must accept the grace bestowed upon us freely as a paddle of redemption in our desert, sea, or Promised Land experience. *"Being justified freely by His grace through the redemption that is in Christ Jesus."* Romans 3:24.

- [ ] We must exhibit calmness and self-control in all we do, say, and become. *"Whom God set forth as a propitiation by His blood, through faith, to demonstrate His righteousness, because in His forbearance God had passed over the sins that were previously committed."* Romans 3:25.

- [ ] We must follow a straight and narrow path of justice and righteousness. *"To demonstrate at the present time His righteousness, that He might be just and the justifier of the one who has faith in Jesus."* Romans 3:26.

- [ ] We do not need to brag, boosting our self-esteem, because we are all blessed to be a blessing. *"Where is boasting then? It is excluded. By what law? Of works? No, but by the law of faith."* Romans 3:27.

- [ ] Our liberation comes through faithful and consistent Fruits of the Spirit and Christlike Character instead of vain repetition of works to show off. *"Therefore we conclude that a man is justified by faith apart from the deeds of the law."* Romans 3:28.

☐ We must understand that God is available to all, regardless of our creed, deed, or breed. *"Or is He the God of the Jews only? Is He not also the God of the Gentiles? Yes, of the Gentiles also."* Romans 3:29.

☐ We must understand that God will remove anything or anyone unpleasing to Him, or not conducive to us. *"Since there is one God who will justify the circumcised by faith and the uncircumcised through faith."* Romans 3:30.

☐ We must understand that we cannot blot out God's Laws, Principles, and Concepts because we are all One, establishing and completing the Purpose for which we were created in the first place. *"Do we then make void the law through faith? Certainly not! On the contrary, we establish the law."* Romans 3:31.

Now, before I move on, as it relates to the *Heavenly of Heavens*, let me break down the Spiritual DNA from my perspective, opening our Spiritual Eyes to what is really happening. The DNA of the Spirit is our *Divine Navigational Apparatus*. It is designed to assist us in getting to the Destiny Enriched Provision to finance, train, extract, trigger, position, or propel us into our Divine Destiny. In this process, if our character is half-keeled or our fruits are spoiled, we may miss out, miss the mark, or have to go back to the drawing board or Spiritual Classroom for regrafting. Unfortunately, this is where many people give up, choosing to embrace their worldly DNA instead of their Spiritual DNA.

Listen, regardless of where we are in life, we are all here for a reason, and if we do not know this valuable information, we cannot fully capitalize on it as we should. Why can we not capitalize, especially if we are Bloodwashed Believers? We will be limited regardless of what we believe when we operate in selfishness as opposed to selflessness. In my opinion, it is similar to our perception to please ourselves or our agenda versus the Perception of God, operating *As It Pleases Him.*

When it comes down to our Bloodline Profile, we must understand the DNA of Godliness versus the DNA of ungodliness. What is the purpose of knowing the difference, especially as Believers? To ensure we do not get caught straddling in the middle of whatever without a paddle to get out. Nevertheless, all is not lost; let us go deeper.

If we take a moment to evaluate our Spiritual Anatomy (our framework) instead of the Physical, we will find that its composition is unmatched. Our material Physical Anatomy can be seen, whereas our immaterial Spiritual, Soulish, and Mental Anatomy cannot, making the three unseen divisions more powerful than the one seen. Is this Biblical? Well, as it relates to *The Great Reveal*, let us take it to scripture: *"For You formed my inward parts; You covered me in my mother's womb. I will praise You, for I am fearfully and wonderfully made; Marvelous are Your works, and that my soul knows very well. My frame was not hidden from You, when I was made in secret, and skillfully wrought in the lowest parts of the earth. Your eyes saw my substance, being yet unformed. And in Your book they all were written, the days fashioned for me, when as yet there were none of them."* Psalm 139:13-16. *"Do you not know that your body is the temple of the Holy Spirit who is in you, whom you have from God, and you are not your own? For you were bought at a price; therefore glorify God in your body and in your spirit, which are God's."* 1 Corinthians 6:19-20.

Why do we need to know this information? The fall of man from Genesis to Revelation has always been from within the human psyche (the mind and soul), affecting the Spirit. We can tiptoe around this, but within the pit of our belly (our core), we know the truth. And, if we deny it, Spiritual Healing cannot take place as it should, possibly causing our Spirit to lie dormant. Why would this happen to us, especially when loving and praising God? We become lukewarm, treading the fence in our Spirituality with disobedience, debauchery, rotten fruits, and cluelessness. At the same time, we are not truly understanding what is really happening around us from a Spiritual Perspective.

From the beginning of time, the battle has always been with our bloodline (our DNA), period. But more importantly, it has not changed. The illusion of viruses and craters of the end time, the apocalyptic era, is similar to our red blood cells carrying oxygen through the body. And the white blood cells fight off illnesses, viruses, and harmful bacteria, which definitely keeps us alive. If the cells in our blood turn on each other, or if our platelets do not clot to stop bleeding, we will have health problems, period.

What is more, if we become deprived of oxygen, we turn blue, or if we die, we turn dark (blackish blue), disconnecting us from this world. What does this mean? It is water and oxygen that create the bridge in our earthly or Heavenly experience that is working desperately to keep us here or take us out.

Humanly, our blood seems to be the most vital link we have to live a fulfilled life, but it is not! It is the elements of who we are from the inside out that have the Spiritual Power needed for a time such as this. Am I pulling for straws? Absolutely not! Our soul is essential to God, for the Bible says, *"For the life of the flesh is in the blood, and I have given it to you upon the altar to make atonement for your souls; for it is the blood that makes atonement for the soul."* Leviticus 17:11.

Why would God make atonement for us? According to the *Heavenly of Heavens*, the same way our blood redeems and connects us to life, our Mind, Soul, and Spirit connect us back to the Source from which we were created. For example, first, if we look at our Soul as red blood cells, the vehicle giving life. Secondly, our Mind is the vehicle to fight off infections of the Soul. And, thirdly, our Spirit becomes the platelets, keeping the Vicissitudes of Life from affecting the Mind and Soul, preventing them from oozing all over the place. With this analogy or mental picture, although appearing gruesome, we can better understand the role of the Holy Spirit.

What is the role of the Holy Spirit? He is vital in correcting, building, guiding, teaching, regulating, and connecting us back to our Creator or the *Heavenly of Heavens* while helping to protect our Bloodline (our DNA structure).

If our Mind, Soul, and Spirit begin to war from within, it is reflected in the BODY. Even if we think we are healthy, our bodies will tell a different story based on the level of warring taking place from within. How can we make this make sense? When our minds or thoughts are unhealthy, we will begin to experience weird things within our bodies. If our Soul is unhealthy, it will begin to absorb all types of conscious or unconscious catalytic contributors of hidden or open traumas to further digress our condition, soul tie us, or keep us in bondage. At the same time, our Spirit is lying dormant, waiting for us to come to ourselves or to awaken from our slumber.

How is it possible to wake up our Spirit when it is not sleeping? If our Spirit is Awake, then we must seek Divine Order in *The Great Reveal*. Let us align this appropriately as it relates to Divine Order from the *Heavenly of Heavens* to create the Spiritual Seal of our Divine Navigational Apparatus. *"This is He who came by water and blood—Jesus Christ; not only by water, but by water and blood. And it is the Spirit who bears witness, because the Spirit is truth. For there are three that bear witness in heaven: the Father, the Word, and the Holy Spirit; and these three are one. And there are three that bear witness on earth: the Spirit, the water, and the blood; and these three agree as one. If we receive the witness of men, the witness of God is greater; for this is the witness of God which He has testified of His Son. He who believes in the Son of God has the witness in himself; he who does not believe God has made Him a liar, because he has not believed the testimony that God has given of His Son. And this is the testimony: that God has given us Eternal Life, and this life is in His Son. He who has the Son has life; he who does not have the Son of God does not have life. These things I have written to you who believe in the name of the Son of God, that you may know that you have Eternal Life, and that you may continue to believe in the name of the Son of God. Now this is the confidence that we have in Him, that if we ask anything according to His will, He hears us."* 1 John 6:-14.

According to the *Heavenly of Heavens*, we must change the way we think, perceive, and dialect with God, ourselves, and others. How do we change when everyone proclaims to have the answer, only for it to become a money grab or disappointment? We must allow ourselves to think inside, outside, around, through, over, and under the box to become a *Spiritual Sensation* of our past, present, and future, *As It Pleases Him*. All other ways outside of God, our Heavenly Father, are hogwash full of fluff and stuff, leading us back to Him in due season! Is this not a little insensitive and biased? Maybe or maybe not, but when your loved ones are yoked to the core, and you are clueless about what to do, and why, trust me, you will thank me for unveiling the TRUTH. I wish I had this information when I was younger; it would have saved me a lot of Battle Scars.

Nevertheless, now that I have the Battle Scars full of Divine Wisdom, Understanding, and Power, let us learn from them, *As It Pleases God*. Listed below are a few ways of expanding ourselves from the inside out. Keep in mind, when using this method, they can work both positively and negatively. So, exercise extreme caution, keeping them on the positive side of the spectrum.

- *Divergent Thinking* is using our imagination to expand upon other possibilities. Using this way of thinking produces ideas, concepts, systems, strategies, and ideologies, giving us the ability to brainstorm from a natural, worldly, different, or Spiritual Perspective.

  Spiritually, this is the *'questioning'* phase of problem-solving or a way of sparking our multi-layered Creativity or Vision. If one needs to create a Mind Map or Spiritual Journal to capture the information during this process, then so be it. Doing so helps us capitalize on our triggered ideas, feelings, behaviors, or thoughts on paper; therefore, giving us the ability to elaborate or connect while enhancing the way we think, believe, perceive, or operate.

- *Convergent Thinking* is using our logical way of receiving, gathering, or unblocking factual truths. In addition, this process helps us create mental analytics from the inside out while helping us connect the dots to our Spiritual Senses.

By far, this is the *'answering'* phase of getting the data needed to solve a problem, make a decision, or come to a rational conclusion. If we position ourselves to receive the right answers, we will learn how to ask better questions, cutting through the hogwash designed to sift us Mentally, Physically, Emotionally, and Spiritually.

☐ *Lateral Thinking* is our ability to use both *Divergent and Convergent Thinking* to take action, become intellectual, or increase our mental activity. Unbeknown to most, this way of thinking helps create brain activity similar to listening to stimulating music or viewing thought-provoking images and quotes.

Now, if we combine positive thinking, listening, and images, we are able to force our mind to work on our behalf, keeping it from forming cobwebs, becoming stuck, or limited. By far, for where God is taking us, we need this one in conjunction with our *Spiritual Thinking* to create a Christlike Personality, yielding the Fruits of the Spirit.

However, if our mind becomes cluttered, stressed, negative, or confused in this phase, it limits our abilities; therefore, we must find a way to relax, pray, or meditate.

☐ *Spiritual Thinking* uses the Biblical Principles and the Spiritual Laws of God in sealing, ushering, or denouncing. The only way to tap into the Mind of God is through the Holy Spirit; therefore, we must understand what the Word of God has to say first. Why? We must do our part!

If God has given us the answers about certain people, places, and things, then why would we ask again for what He has already given? If we take the time to master the Book of Psalms and Proverbs, we will understand the Mind of God from His point of view. However, in this phase, a Mind Map or Spiritual Journal to capture the information during this process is mandatory for *The Great Reveal*.

Does God really require all of this thinking from us? Absolutely not. He did not create us as robots; nevertheless, according to our DNA constructs, the thinking process will occur, but most often in a negative and non-conducive manner. Based on the Spiritual Law of Duality, the goal is to reverse-engineer our thinking patterns from negative to positive, from bad to good, from unwise to wise, and so on, adding God into the equation, *As It Pleases Him*, to prepare ourselves for *The Great Reveal*.

Chapter 8

THE GREAT REVEAL

The Divine Revelation of God is the most sought-after information known to man. Why is it so sought after, especially when having free will and a mind to think rationally? We all have an inner desire to be 'In The Know' about what God is up to, regardless of our System of Belief. Unfortunately, in the Eye of God, this secret longing is not often appropriately channeled, resulting in our partaking of what sounds, looks, or feels good, as well as what gives us dominance without giving a second thought about what PLEASES HIM.

Although we are human with fleshly wants, desires, and urges with a natural desire to dominate, it does not give us the Spiritual Right to omit our Creator. According to the Heavenly of Heavens, for the *Great Reveal*, if we do not exhibit some form of self-control in our known or unknown quest for whatever or whomever, we can become sifted, fulfilling the Spiritual Contradictions while thinking we are right in our own eyes.

More importantly, no one is exempt from the Spiritual Phase of domination and contradictions. Why are we not exempt as Believers, who are actively pursuing the Will of God, covered by the Blood of Jesus, and led by the Holy Spirit? It is in our nature, the nature of the BEAST, to be exact. Simply put, the Spirit of Duality, good and evil, resides within us all and must be tamed, *As It Pleases God*. If not, it will dominate us through the psyche with lies, selfishness, and deception. Nonetheless, the problem comes into play when we REFUSE to become a work-in-progress, learning, growing, and sowing back into the Kingdom of God, *As It Pleases Him*.

Life is the best Spiritual Teacher, but for some odd reason, we try to avoid the Spiritual Lessons or Protocols while trying to obtain the Benefits of the Kingdom. Here is what Hebrews 5:12-14 advises: *"For though by this time you ought to be teachers, you need someone to teach you again the first principles of the Oracles of God; and you have come to need milk and not solid food. For everyone who partakes only of milk is unskilled in the word of righteousness, for he is a babe. But solid food belongs to those who are of full age, that is, those who by reason of use have their senses exercised to discern both good and evil."*

The Great Reveal is wrapped in our ability to understand that we are Heirs of the Kingdom of Heaven. Our Birthright, Promises, and Inheritances from God are contingent on our thoughts, words, behaviors, attitudes, demeanor, actions, reactions, and perceptions. How is this possible? Suppose we are not consistently regrafting our negatives to positives and our ungodly to Godly, creating a win-win. In this case, we can miss the mark, cause a delay in taking possession, or become a victim of the Spiritual Placebos.

What are Spiritual Placebos? They are the Spiritual Counterfeits and wolves in sheep's clothing. Are they not the same? No, they are not, but one person can possess both character traits. Nonetheless, the wolf is intentional, and the Spiritual Counterfeits usually lack the know-how and understanding of Spiritual Authenticity, Anointing, or Oil, *As It Pleases God*.

The Spiritual Counterfeits appearing to be Heaven-Sent are those who see, hear, and speak about people, places, and things from their perspective, bearing little or no Fruits of the Spirit, especially behind closed doors. In addition, it is also those who manipulate the Word of God to benefit their ulterior, ungodly motives. Now, with time, they will eventually lose their effectiveness due to their lack of substance or inconsistency. Is this Biblical? Well, let us take it to scripture, which says, *"For those who live according to the flesh set their minds on the things of the flesh, but those who live according to the Spirit, the things of the Spirit. For to be carnally minded is death, but to be spiritually minded is life and peace. Because the carnal mind is enmity against God; for it is not subject to the law of God, nor indeed can be. So then, those who are in the flesh cannot please God. But you are not in the flesh but in the Spirit, if indeed the Spirit of God dwells in you. Now if anyone does not have the Spirit of Christ, he is not His."* Romans 8:5-9.

How can we determine a Spiritual Counterfeit? Once again, we are known by our fruits, as well as our character traits. When we misrepresent ourselves and the Kingdom of God, with dark motives, impacting or manipulating the innocent, rest assured, counterfeit schemes are at play. Here is the deal: No one is exempt from this charactorial glitch or trigger. If we proclaim that we are, then we are lying to ourselves; it only takes the right conditions to unveil it. Fortunately, this is one of the reasons we need self-control to tame or calm this hidden beast.

At the core of a Spiritual Counterfeit's behavior, there are a few specific items to take note of when it comes down to Spiritual Placebos, but not limited to such:

- ☐ A Spiritual Counterfeit is known by their thwarted, coerced, or debriefed Spiritual Vision of hostile aggression. Simply put, they are control freaks!

- ☐ A Spiritual Counterfeit is known by their lovelessness or concealed biases due to conditioning or hidden traumas.

- ☐ A Spiritual Counterfeit is known by their hopelessness and negativity. All of which are concealed by the desire to be accepted by someone or a group of people.

- ☐ A Spiritual Counterfeit is known by judging the worth of others without knowing them or asking fact-finding questions to cover up their hidden insecurities.

- ☐ A Spiritual Counterfeit is known by their sealed or one-way mindset or thinking patterns. All of which are derived from their pompousness, disobedience, disrespectfulness, and lack of direction.

- ☐ A Spiritual Counterfeit is known by their aiding in the tribulations and downfall of others. Then again, they are savvy in creating known or unknown curses within their Bloodline or pronouncing ill will over the innocent to satiate their interests.

- ☐ A Spiritual Counterfeit is known by their blowing the trumpet on others, ratting them out, or degrading those who have genuinely helped them. Simply put, they lack loyalty.

- ☐ A Spiritual Counterfeit is known by their selling out the Kingdom of God for fame, money, status, power, clicks, likes, and prestige.

- ☐ A Spiritual Counterfeit is known by using excessive terms of endearment, words like baby, love, honey, sweetheart, beloved, dear, or precious to manipulate, connive, and scheme. The bottom line is that their actions do not align with what is coming out of their mouth. In addition, they may use or exploit someone's love language against them to get what they want. Once done, they move on without a conscience.

- ☐ A Spiritual Counterfeit is known by their unjust persecution of the innocent or negatively altering their Divine Destiny to benefit their hidden agenda.

- ☐ A Spiritual Counterfeit loses their Voice of Righteousness to unrighteous coercion, bribing, pimping, and scheming to pad their pockets.

- ☐ A Spiritual Counterfeit is known by their demigod thinking and behaving. They are psychologically convinced that their demands and prayers are above God's Divine Will.

- ☐ A Spiritual Counterfeit is known by their intermingling with false gods, or interjecting paganism into their prayers to shift the Spiritual Atmosphere of the Righteous for an unrighteous cause.

How can we break the Spiritual Placebos? According to scripture, it says, "*I will take up the cup of salvation, and call upon the Name of the Lord. I will pay my vows to the Lord now in the presence of all His people.*" Psalm 116:12-14. What does this mean for Believers? We must humbly redeem ourselves before God and others with clean hands and a pure heart as an Oath of Redemption, *As It Pleases Him*, renouncing our selfishness or thwarted agendas of pleasing ourselves or our ego.

Divine Spirituality, *As It Pleases God*, is all about being Spiritually Authentic instead of allowing ourselves to become self-aggrandizing and inauthentic. Plus, we cannot willfully strike down God's Chosen Elect for not bending to our will. Listen, there are consequences and repercussions for those who unjustifiably strike others, Mentally, Physically, Emotionally, or Spiritually, who are Divinely Covered and Truly Righteous in the Sight of God.

If we unjustifiably contend with the Spiritually Chosen Vessels who are in Purpose on purpose, we must search our motives carefully. If we err in this formality, the Wrath of God will come down upon our heads so fast that it will make our heads spin. Therefore, we must exercise extreme caution when knowingly or unknowingly using ungodly prayers to strike down the Godly.

What is the reason for such caution, especially when contending with Chosen Ones? It will cause our prayers to backfire on us, our children, a family member, or someone in our bloodline. Then again, it may outright create a generational curse, especially if we know better and choose not to do better.

For God's Chosen Elect, we are held to a higher standard, period! When we are trained in the ways of God by the Holy Spirit, if we allow arrogance or disobedience to convolute our Spiritual Training, then unfortunately, the Rod of Correction will prevail.

For example, we can all relate to Moses, who led the Israelites out of bondage and was given the 10 Commandments by God. Yes, in a moment of travailing perils in Numbers 20, the Children of Israel became thirsty. God instructed Moses to speak to the rock so it could yield water; instead, he struck the rock not only once but twice, and water came gushing out. Listen, arrogance, secret anger, rebellion, and disobedience will cause us to strike or lash out at people, places, and things when we are ordained to speak to them.

What is the problem, especially when they received water anyway? The problem is that Moses DID NOT follow instructions, becoming irritated, reasserting his human nature into what was Divine. When we seek to impose our dominance over people without exhibiting humility, rest assured that correction will occur.

Although Moses had success previously in Exodus 14:5-6 with striking, his attitude was totally different back then. Here is the scripture, *"And the LORD said to Moses, 'Go on before the people, and take with you some of the elders of Israel. Also take in your hand your rod with which you struck the river, and go. Behold, I will stand before you there on the rock in Horeb; and you shall strike the rock, and water will come out of it, that the people may drink.' And Moses did so in the sight of the elders of Israel."*

Once we have a track record of miracles, it can become easy to want to have and do things our way or make assumptions outright. Whereas God does not want us to assume anything, we need to become truth seekers, putting our negative, deceiving thoughts and emotions in their rightful place of correctability. What does this mean? If we cannot stand to be corrected, we may have communication issues, preventing us from hearing the instructions of God clearly or *As It Pleases Him*.

Just so we are clear, casting down evil to protect ourselves is our Spiritual Right. Whereas, justly or unjustly *'striking down'* someone to control, manipulate, or rule over them for ungodly means, violating their free will...unfortunately, this is a form of witchcraft, regardless of how we rationalize or justify our behavior. In *The Great Reveal*, we need to be careful and wise with our prayers, our leisurely spoken words, and our casual thoughts. Luke 6:45 explains the reasons why: *"A good man out of the good treasure of his heart brings forth good; and an evil man out of the evil treasure of his heart brings forth evil. For out of the abundance of the heart his mouth speaks."*

What if someone is degradingly evil towards us? As a Kingdom Builder, we do not need to become likewise, getting out of character. Here is what the Bible has to say about this: *"Finally, all of you be of one mind, having compassion for one another; love as brothers, be tenderhearted, be courteous; not returning evil for evil or reviling for reviling, but on the contrary blessing, knowing that you were called to this, that you may inherit a blessing. For He who would love life and see good days, let him refrain his tongue from evil, and his lips from speaking deceit."* 1 Peter 3:8-10. In addition, it asks, *"Who is wise and understanding among you? Let him show by good conduct that his works are done in the meekness of wisdom."* James 3:13.

Just so we are clear, a few rotten fruits, weaknesses, or habits do not make us counterfeit, especially if we become a work-in-progress, owning our truth, while truly becoming better to create a win-win for the Kingdom without deceiving God, ourselves, and others. How do we exercise wisdom in this matter? We must pay attention to two things:

- ☐ *"The wisdom that is from above is first pure, then peaceable, gentle, willing to yield, full of mercy and good fruits, without partiality and without hypocrisy. Now the fruit of righteousness is sown in peace by those who make peace."* James 3:17-18.

- ☐ *"But if you have bitter envy and self-seeking in your hearts, do not boast and lie against the truth. This wisdom does not descend from above, but is earthly, sensual, and demonic. For where envy and self-seeking exist, confusion and every evil thing are there."* James 3:14-16.

Even if we need to make out a list of Godly Character Traits versus the ungodly ones, then so be it. If we are not accustomed to thinking, behaving, and speaking positively, we may not recognize the differences. We often take the positive versus the negative for granted, but some people may NOT have been conditioned to know the difference. How do I know? I was one of those people! I was very naive back in the day, but through God's Grace and Mercy, the Spiritual Classroom has proven itself to work on my behalf, serving the Kingdom of God to become a Messenger of the Good News.

Now that I know the difference between positive and negative, it has been designed by the Heavenly of Heavens to make my *GIVE BACK* epic! No one knows my story better than I do; therefore, I take nothing for granted. Why not? What is common for one person may not be common for the next, especially when our commonalities or so-called common sense have us yoked, soul-tied, bound, or veiled. So, when it comes down to *The Great Reveal*, I break down the Spiritual Revelations to *Unveil the Veiled* in Earthen Vessel, pulling back the layers of superficialities of our yesterday. What does this mean? We are outing the old, ushering in the fresh, unadulterated Word of God to heal the weary soul for such a time as this.

Before we go any further, let me put my spin on Reveal for a moment. If I read Reveal in reverse, it says laever (lever). So, my goal is to pull the Spiritual Lever on the veiled, opening our Spiritual Eyes, Ears, and Mouth to the Kingdom of Heaven, bridging the Spiritual Gaps holding us back from the Divine. How do we know if we are veiled? Listed below are a few correlations between the veiled and Spiritually Unveiled, but not limited to such:

- ☐ If we are Selfish versus Unselfish.
- ☐ If we are Self-Willed versus God-Willed.
- ☐ If we are Condemnatory versus Understanding.
- ☐ If we are Unmerciful versus Merciful.
- ☐ If we are Cruel versus Kind.
- ☐ If we are Unforgiving versus Forgiving.
- ☐ If we are Prideful versus Humble.

- ☐ If we are Abrasive versus Gentle.
- ☐ If we are Combative versus Peaceable.
- ☐ If we are Rude versus Respectful.
- ☐ If we are Out of Control versus Self-Controlled.
- ☐ If we are Self-Conscious versus God-Conscious.

Just so we are clear, veiled or not, staying on the positive side of the spectrum, Mentally, Physically, Emotionally, and Spiritually takes work, period. Positivity works for the just and unjust alike, outside of having a Spiritual Relationship with our Heavenly Father. *"For there is no partiality with God."* Romans 2:11. Unfortunately, this is why we have more positive worldly people than we have in the Kingdom of God. Blasphemy, right? Wrong. If we stop lying to ourselves, we will find that positive, worldly individuals live a more fulfilled life than those who are sold out for Jesus.

As it relates to *The Great Reveal*, we will find those proclaiming to be in the Kingdom are lashing out at the worldly because God has shown them more favor. But more importantly, those who are supposed to have a Kingdom Mindset are by no means able to control their jealousy, envy, covetousness, greed, pride, and bullying tactics, spewing it all over those appearing to be more blessed than they are.

In all actuality, from God's Divine Perspective, we are ALL blessed to be a blessing. What is more, in or out of the Kingdom, with negative unrestrained thoughts, behaviors, and emotions, the mind becomes the enemy's playground, yoking us to and fro without us having a clue about what is taking place. Yet, we continue to lie to ourselves, especially when the psyche is having a field day, causing us to overlook our blessings and become riddled with ungratefulness.

According to the Heavenly of Heavens, we have more dream-killers in the church than we have in the secular world. So today, as a part of *The Great Reveal*, the lies stop here!

When our negative characteristics outweigh the positive or if we are a secret dream killer, we must consider the Spiritual

Regrafting Process to grow, sow, and do more for the Kingdom. For this reason, we must get the Holy Trinity (The Father, Son, and Holy Spirit) involved in this process to reel us in Mentally, Physically, Emotionally, and Spiritually. Why can we not do this on our own? We can. We have free will to choose whatever we so desire; however, I must advise that this is a God-Ruled Nation with Spiritual Protocol, Laws, and Precepts governing our Spiritual Matters.

Why do we need the Holy Trinity in Spiritual Matters? The Holy Trinity creates the Spiritual Counterbalancing needed to keep us in alignment with Divine Order, our Purpose, or Governing the use of our Gifts, Calling, Creativity, and Talents. Just keep in mind that if we become idolistically pompous, controlling God Almighty, we may lose a few notches off our belt, and the last thing we need is a Spiritual Beat-Down from the inside out.

More importantly, when doing so, there are Spiritual Rules upholding our Spiritual Standards in the Kingdom that we need to know. What are they? There are many, but let us begin here; it says, *"Remind them to be subject to rulers and authorities, to obey, to be ready for every good work, to speak evil of no one, to be peaceable, gentle, showing all humility to all men."* Titus 3:1-2. Why do we need to behave in such a manner when we are surrounded by chaos, confusion, and drama? *"For we ourselves were also once foolish, disobedient, deceived, serving various lusts and pleasures, living in malice and envy, hateful and hating one another."* Titus 3:3.

How can we regraft ourselves for *The Great Reveal*? First, it is done transparently and truthfully, *As It Pleases God*, and not to please ourselves. Secondly, scripturally: *"But when the kindness and the love of God our Savior toward man appeared, not by works of righteousness which we have done, but according to His mercy He saved us, through the washing of regeneration and renewing of the Holy Spirit, whom He poured out on us abundantly through Jesus Christ our Savior, that having been justified by His grace we should become heirs according to the hope of Eternal Life."* Titus 3:4-7.

Why do we need the Holy Spirit in this process? First, He helps us to avoid or deal with worldliness from the inside out, *As It Pleases*

God. Secondly, He prevents us from getting out of character and exhibiting foolery. Here is what we need to know: *"Avoid foolish disputes, genealogies, contentions, and strivings about the law; for they are unprofitable and useless. Reject a divisive man after the first and second admonition, knowing that such a person is warped and sinning, being self-condemned."* Titus 3:9-11.

Just so we are clear, we are required to become a Spiritual Lamp to the world, but if someone is hell-bent on destroying our light or traumatizing us, we need to kindly back up with a smile on our faces. We cannot violate the free will of another. If we force our light on others, it becomes dim by default. How is this possible when we are doing the Work of God? We are designed to share the Good News, allowing God to do the rest without allowing darkness, hatefulness, or waywardness to sift, traumatize, torture, abuse, bully, or destroy us. We must keep it moving in the Spirit of Excellence, similar to how Jesus kept moving, without allowing the naysayers to thwart the Mission of God.

Should we not fight for God? Yes, we should fight with the Good Fight of Faith. But I have a question, 'Do we think God is weak or a wimp and cannot hold His own?' The best fight for the Kingdom is using the Fruits of the Spirit and behaving Christlike, period! What if we appear weak? Weakness is a matter of perception.

Nevertheless, in the Eye of God, without self-control, *As It Pleases Him*, it is an automatic defeat and back to the drawing board! How? Once again, the fight is within! The enemy will target us Mentally, Emotionally, or Spiritually, extending outwardly to the Physical to spoil our fruits and create doubt or provoke us to engage in foolery.

Listen, if people reject us, our good fruits, or our Christlike Character, we must move on to those who are open to receiving our fresh Fruits of the Spirit. Really? Yes, really. *"For the grace of God that brings salvation has appeared to all men, teaching us that, denying ungodliness and worldly lusts, we should live soberly, righteously, and godly in the present age, looking for the blessed hope and glorious appearing of our great God and Savior Jesus Christ, who gave Himself for us, that He might redeem us from every lawless deed and purify for Himself His own special people, zealous for good works." Titus 2:11-14.*

What is God expecting in our good works? God expects us to begin our good works by exhibiting the Fruits of the Spirit (Love, Joy, Peace, Patience, Kindness, Goodness, Faithfulness, Gentleness, and Self-Control) and Christlike Character. Once we Spiritually Graduate from this level, God will take us to the next one.

Can we get to the next level without God, the Fruits of the Spirit, or Christlike Character? Yes, but we must go to the dark side to get it while nullifying the use of the Blood of Jesus as our Sacrificial Lamb for our Spiritual Atonement. What does this mean? We must make other types of sacrifices to appeal to the dark side or other gods. As a word of caution, we may not like the sacrificial requirements, so be very careful. Frankly, some of the generational curses coming along with venturing to the dark side cannot be UNDONE until they run their course through our Bloodline. So, we must determine if that is the price we want to pay for temporary gratification or shortcuts to please ourselves.

If we stay with God, we must follow the proper Spiritual Protocol of Spiritual Training. If we are not able to exhibit the Fruits of the Spirit, we cannot exhibit authentic Christlike Character without having ulterior motives.

Most often, when we avoid Spiritual Protocol, we tend to fall into the category of making God more scientific (explainable) as opposed to Spiritually Absolute (complete and unchanging). Nevertheless, for the church or the Spiritual Elites, according to scripture, the qualities of *The Great Reveal* are:

- ☐ *"But as for you, speak the things which are proper for sound doctrine: that the older men be sober, reverent, temperate, sound in faith, in love, in patience."* Titus 2:1-2.

- ☐ *"The older women likewise, that they be reverent in behavior, not slanderers, not given to much wine, teachers of good things—that they admonish the young women to love their husbands, to love their Children."* Titus 2:3-4.

- ☐ "To be discreet, chaste, homemakers, good, obedient to their own husbands, that the word of God may not be blasphemed." Titus 2:5.

- ☐ "Likewise, exhort the young men to be sober-minded, in all things showing yourself to be a pattern of good works; in doctrine showing integrity, reverence, incorruptibility, sound speech that cannot be condemned, that one who is an opponent may be ashamed, having nothing evil to say of you." Titus 2:6-8.

- ☐ "Exhort bondservants to be obedient to their own masters, to be well pleasing in all things, not answering back, not pilfering, but showing all good fidelity, that they may adorn the doctrine of God our Savior in all things." Titus 2:9-10.

- ☐ "For the grace of God that brings salvation has appeared to all men, teaching us that, denying ungodliness and worldly lusts, we should live soberly, righteously, and godly in the present age, looking for the blessed hope and glorious appearing of our great God and Savior Jesus Christ, who gave Himself for us, that He might redeem us from every lawless deed and purify for Himself His own special people, zealous for good works." Titus 2:11-14.

- ☐ "Speak these things, exhort, and rebuke with all authority. Let no one despise you." Titus 2:15.

In *The Great Reveal*, God is looking for worthiness from the inside out, not from the outside in. What is the big deal, especially when we are not perfect and are saved by grace? Grace cannot keep us if we knowingly or unknowingly curse ourselves due to a lack of understanding or knowledge.

Of course, we all make mistakes and need grace and mercy. But our fruits and character tell a different story to God, unveiling our true motives or heart posture. The enemy only needs one open door to sift us; therefore, our hearts and motives must be pure to contend when we err. If not, we will 'get got' by the enemy's wiles or turn on ourselves from the inside out.

What do we need to do to purify our hearts? According to scripture, *"For a bishop must be blameless, as a steward of God, not self-willed, not quick-tempered, not given to wine, not violent, not greedy for money, but hospitable, a lover of what is good, sober-minded, just, holy, self-controlled, holding fast the faithful word as he has been taught, that he may be able, by sound doctrine, both to exhort and convict those who contradict."* Titus 1:7-9. Why do we need all of this for *The Great Reveal*? Our faith is under scrutiny. By whom?

- ☐ Those who aim to deceive, manipulate, and bully others. *"For there are many insubordinate, both idle talkers and deceivers, especially those of the circumcision."* Titus 1:10.

- ☐ Those who pride themselves on breaking up the homes of others. *"Whose mouths must be stopped, who subvert whole households, teaching things which they ought not, for the sake of dishonest gain."* Titus 1:11.

- ☐ Those who are stereotyping. *"One of them, a prophet of their own, said, Cretans (A Certain People Stereotype) are always liars, evil beasts, and lazy gluttons."* Titus 1:12.

- ☐ Those who destroy others with their mouth. *"This testimony is true. Therefore rebuke them sharply, that they may be sound in the faith."* Titus 1:13.

- ☐ Those who judge or discredit the Word of God. *"Not giving heed to Jewish fables and commandments of men who turn from the truth."* Titus 1:14.

- ☐ Those who are hurt, hurt others. *"To the pure all things are pure, but to those who are defiled and unbelieving nothing is pure; but even their mind and conscience are defiled."* Titus 1:15.

- ☐ Those who are false prophets. *"They profess to know God, but in works they deny Him, being abominable, disobedient, and disqualified for every good work."* Titus 1:16.

As a part of *The Great Reveal*, all is not lost. According to the Heavenly of Heavens, we have work to do, *As It Pleases God*, opening our Spiritual Eyes, Ears, and Mouth to make a bold declaration similar to Paul in 2 Timothy 4:6-8. It says, *"For I am already being poured out as a drink offering, and the time of my departure is at hand. I have fought the good fight, I have finished the race, I have kept the faith. Finally, there is laid up for me the crown of righteousness, which the Lord, the righteous Judge, will give to me on that Day, and not to me only but also to all who have loved His appearing."*

The Great Reveal requires us to *"Preach the word! Be ready in season and out of Season."* 2 Timothy, 4:2. How? This book is designed to create readiness from the inside out, the way God intended, *As It Pleases Him*. Therefore, one must take heed.

God is faithful, and He wants us to become filled with faith as well, taking advantage of the blessed seeds of our cause-and-effect (seedtime and harvest) Spiritual Relationship. We cannot go wrong serving Him with clean hands, a pure heart, and a wholesome conscience. God is reliable and unchanging, especially when it comes down to the Blessings, Birthrights, and Promises of the Righteous Chosen Elect.

If we want all God has to offer, an in-depth examination must occur from the inside out. Furthermore, we must up the ante on our perspectives and their associations with our thoughts, behaviors, personality, conditioning, inner conflicts, outer influences, and free will.

On the other hand, if we do not understand ourselves, it becomes difficult to understand God's Secrets and much easier to violate another's will due to our unrealized selfishness. How is this possible when we are devout believers? We are created in the Image of God, which means we are One with our Heavenly Father, but it DOES NOT mean we are COMPLETE In Him. We must Spiritually Till our own ground using the Fruits of the Spirit and behaving Christlike.

In taking this a step further, if we have not honed in on the *Spirit to Spirit* Relationship with God, we are NOT granted all access to the Kingdom. Why are we deprived of Divine Access? We may become reckless, hurting ourselves, abusing others, and misrepresenting the Kingdom more than helping, especially if we are not adequately covered by the Blood of Jesus and guided by the Holy Spirit. Suppose we omit the Holy Trinity (The Father, Son, and Holy Spirit) in our Spiritual Relationship. In this case, we will become selfish by default. Plus, we will also miss out on the Spiritual Shaping and Character Building process needed for us to become rooted and grounded in Kingdom Principles, Laws, and Pristineness, *As It Pleases God.*

Intermittent Spirituality is not going to get us a seat at the Spiritual Table. Why not, as long as we are serving God, this should be enough, right? Unfortunately, it makes us wishy-washy, unreliable, and selfish. Besides, who wants to walk on eggshells when we are around someone? I know I do not!

Sporadic Spirituality is unwise and dangerous. Whereas, Consistent Spirituality builds authenticity, comfort, reliability, and trust. Of course, no one is perfect in this area...The difference is the ability to self-correct at the drop of a dime.

How can we break our intermittency? Suppose we use the Fruits of the Spirit consistently, correcting ourselves when erring, repenting, and creating a win-win while reapplying the use of positive fruits when falling short. In this case, it gives us staying or standing power to observe ourselves. Does this work? Absolutely! It does not make us perfect; it makes us Spiritually Aware of what we are doing, saying, and becoming, as well as the reasons why. Doing so ensures that we are not walking around exhibiting clueless behavior, bringing forth spoiled rotten fruit, or contaminating our Bloodline with undercover bullies. However, we must 'Become Okay' with a few things, but not limited to such:

- ☐ We must 'Become Okay' with not fitting in.
- ☐ We must 'Become Okay' with being misunderstood.
- ☐ We must 'Become Okay' with being openly different or transparent.
- ☐ We must 'Become Okay' with being rejected.
- ☐ We must 'Become Okay' with respecting the opinion or free will of another.
- ☐ We must 'Become Okay' with resistance.
- ☐ We must 'Become Okay' with our quirks and self-awareness.
- ☐ We must 'Become Okay' with being challenged or disciplined.
- ☐ We must 'Become Okay' with not having all the answers or problem-solving.
- ☐ We must 'Become Okay' with saying 'no' or taking calculated risks.
- ☐ We must 'Become Okay' with growing, sowing, sharing, and reaping.
- ☐ We must 'Become Okay' with tapping into the Spiritual Reservoir of Divine Greatness.

As simple as these 'Okay Principles' seem to some, they are profound and undetectable kryptonite for most, creating worldly veils. Is this Biblical? Absolutely! *"Therefore, since we have this ministry, as we have received mercy, we do not lose heart. But we have renounced the hidden things of shame, not walking in craftiness nor handling the word of God deceitfully, but by manifestation of the truth commending ourselves to every man's conscience in the sight of God. But even if our gospel is veiled, it is veiled to those who are perishing, whose minds the god of this age has blinded, who do not believe, lest the light of the gospel of the glory of Christ, who is the image of God, should shine on them. For we do not preach ourselves, but Christ Jesus the*

Lord, and ourselves your bondservants for Jesus' sake. For it is the God who commanded light to shine out of darkness, who has shone in our hearts to give the light of the knowledge of the glory of God in the face of Jesus Christ." Corinthians 4:1-6.

Chapter 9

BULLIES UNVEILED

Our worldly biases, continual judgment, and lack of perseverance are the hidden strongholds on our journey toward our Divine Destiny. They all target our confidence level, causing one to become a known or unknown bully or instigator. If a person chooses not to give, do, or say anything, why should we provoke them, right? This free will violation sets us up to fail in the Kingdom.

We cannot violate the free will of another; we are here to bring the Good News, not force it. Spiritually, our battle is half won when we become a Vessel of God and not a bully for God. The humility engrossed in our Mental, Physical, Emotional, and Spiritual Freedom paves the way to the Kingdom, *As It Pleases God*.

When we are in bondage, yoked, or soul-tied, we will become Spiritually Blind, Deaf, or Mute if we are not fully equipped to break it. Most often, bullies may feel as if the world is unjust in many ways; however, God's Divine Creation is just, serving its Purpose! How do I know? According to scripture, it says: *"But the LORD shall endure forever; He has prepared His throne for judgment. He shall judge the world in righteousness, and He shall administer judgment for the peoples in uprightness."* Psalm 9:7-8. In so many words, we are held accountable, regardless of how we rationalize or justify our behaviors.

Bullies are all around us, and it is sometimes within us without us realizing it. Here is the deal: A bully is someone who habitually seeks to harm, intimidate, or dominate those who are perceived as weaker or vulnerable. More importantly, they use physical or verbal aggression to assert their power and control over others. Then again, they may display a lack of empathy or concern for the feelings and well-being of their victims.

On the other hand, unbeknown to most, a bully will resort to underhanded tactics such as spreading rumors or gossip, excluding or isolating others, and cyberbullying through social media or other online platforms. The bottom line is that bullies create a negative and toxic environment that is DISPLEASING in the Eye of God while thinking this behavior is justified for money, a follower, or a click!

For the record, intentionally causing feelings of anxiety, stress, and discomfort is detrimental to the human psyche; therefore, God does not take this behavior lightly. Nor do we get a free pass for having loose lips or character-assassinating someone publicly to bring about shame.

If we do a self-analysis according to scripture, we have a few types of people whom bullies will target, but not limited to such:

- ☐ Bullies target those who are oppressed.
- ☐ Bullies target those who are hungry from the inside out.
- ☐ Bullies target those who are self-imprisoned.
- ☐ Bullies target those who are blind, deaf, and mute.
- ☐ Bullies target those who are bowed down.
- ☐ Bullies target those who are righteous, following the Will of God.
- ☐ Bullies target those who are strangers in a foreign land.
- ☐ Bullies target those who are fatherless or widows.

Is this Biblical regarding those targeted by bullies? I would have it no other way. According to scripture, it says, *"Who executes justice for the oppressed, who gives food to the hungry. The LORD gives freedom to the prisoners. The LORD opens the eyes of the blind; the LORD raises those who are bowed down; the LORD loves the righteous. The LORD watches over the strangers; He relieves the fatherless and widow; but the way of the wicked He* turns upside down. The LORD shall reign forever—Your God, O Zion, to all generations. Praise the LORD!" Psalm 146:7-10.

Listed below are a few vital Spiritual Principles to keep us 'In-the-Know' about what is on Heaven's Mind:

- ☐ "The LORD upholds all who fall, and raises up all who are bowed down." Psalm 145:14.
- ☐ "The eyes of all look expectantly to You, and You give them their food in due season." Psalm 145:15.
- ☐ "You open Your hand and satisfy the desire of every living thing." Psalm 145:16.
- ☐ "The LORD is righteous in all His ways, gracious in all His works." Psalm 145:17.
- ☐ "The LORD is near to all who call upon Him, to all who call upon Him in truth." Psalm 145:18.
- ☐ "He will fulfill the desire of those who fear Him; He also will hear their cry and save them." Psalm 145:19.
- ☐ "The LORD preserves all who love Him, but all the wicked He will destroy." Psalm 145:20.
- ☐ "My mouth shall speak the praise of the LORD, and all flesh shall bless His holy name Forever and ever." Psalm 145:21.

Why do we need to know these Spiritual Principles? Because we are human, and we are subject to erring on occasion and becoming bullies. In doing so, we have two choices: Remain the same or make a change. Plus, regardless of our choices, we do not want to contaminate our Spiritual Armor by not knowing how God delivers those dealing with specific issues or those feeling like they have been dealt a bad hand.

God wants us to fear Him, not the person who is bribing or bullying; plus, He wants us to become aware of our motives as well. According to Kingdom Principles, bribes are a form of bullying. Really? Yes, really! Here is the scripture, "Now therefore, let the fear of *the LORD be upon you; take care and do it, for there is no iniquity with the LORD our God, no partiality, nor taking of bribes."* 2 Chronicles 19:7. What makes this so important in the Eye of God? Whether we are doing the bullying bribe or accepting it, both are accountable. How is this possible? Let us take it to scripture, *"And you shall take no bribe, for a bribe blinds the discerning and perverts the words of the righteous."* Exodus 23:8.

Contrary to what most would think, those who are shy or not well-spoken are among the biggest bullies or secret stalkers. What is the reason for such? First, most people underestimate their level of aggression or astuteness. Secondly, they are excellent at withholding things, being selfishly withdrawn, playing pretend, or pryingly sneaky. Thirdly, they have become experts in hiding their feelings to cause deprivation to another, or outright holding back their feelings of love. And, fourthly, these are the folks who say 'No' to show another who is really in charge when it is well within their power to say 'Yes.'

Just so we are clear before moving on, no one is exempt from becoming a bully, even if the Holy Trinity is involved. How is this possible? We are not robots; we have free will to do, say, and become whatever we like. The only snag in doing so is the Spiritual Repercussions or Implications. What does this mean? Right is right, wrong is wrong, bullying is bullying, and deception is deception, thus making us accountable for our choices.

It does not matter if we are the instigators or instigatees; bullying is never the answer. Bullies are hurting people who hurt others for their worldly sanctity while recruiting others to do likewise, putting on a show of superficial superiority.

The bottom line is that flexing our muscles or the bullying ego is our conscious mind building a layer of protection for what is really buried unconsciously within. Clearly, this does not make us bad people; however, to become Kingdomly Usable, *As It Pleases God*, we must do a clean sweep on the bully from within.

Even if we are a cautious or carefree bully, once again, we are human, and the bully from within will protect itself from another bully by default! How? It is built into our DNA; therefore, we do not want it to go to the left. For a time such as this, we must become AWARE of it for the INTERNAL REGRAFTING process, *As It Pleases God*. Here is a list of how human we are, but not limited to such:

- ☐ We all have experienced a state of *denial* regarding the truth to protect ourselves.
- ☐ We all have *repressed* or blocked thoughts to protect ourselves.
- ☐ We all have *redirected* our thoughts, words, desires, and emotions to protect ourselves.
- ☐ We all have *suppressed* our thoughts, words, desires, and emotions to protect ourselves.
- ☐ We all have *subdued* our thoughts, words, desires, and emotions to protect ourselves.
- ☐ We all have *regrafted* our thoughts, words, desires, and emotions to protect ourselves.
- ☐ We all have *blocked* our thoughts, words, desires, and emotions to protect ourselves.
- ☐ We all have *channeled* our thoughts, words, desires, and emotions to protect ourselves.
- ☐ We all have *rationalized* our thoughts, words, desires, and emotions to protect ourselves.
- ☐ We all have *corrected* our thoughts, words, desires, and emotions to protect ourselves.
- ☐ We all have *theorized* our thoughts, words, desires, and emotions to protect ourselves.
- ☐ We all have *justified* our thoughts, words, desires, and emotions to protect ourselves.

Why do we need to know this? Regardless of our blessings or shortcomings, we all have an autonomized bully from within. However, it must be adequately controlled; if not, we will have issues from the inside out.

The ringleader bully and dehumanization mentality have been around since the beginning of time. Noah experienced bullies when building the Ark. Yes, the same Ark that God gave him first-hand instructions on how to construct strategically. Yet, the naysayers, dream killers, and bullies came out of the woodwork to thwart the Mission of God.

Just because they could not see the rain coming or lacked Spiritual Vision from the Divine, it did not mean it was not coming! And, due to their lack of understanding, they began spewing their perception over Noah's life to cause him to become as insecure and doubtful as they were.

When we are doing too much to circumvent or discredit a Vessel of God, we must become careful about the consequences and repercussions of our behaviors, thoughts, and perceptions. Picking on or harassing people because we think we are in a position to do so may eventually cause us to become the victim ourselves.

According to the Heavenly of Heavens, a bully is no more than a person who refuses to secretly or openly take responsibility for what they are doing, saying, thinking, or becoming. As a result, they knowingly or unknowingly shift the blame, hurt, trauma, or whatever to others.

In my opinion, most bullies are not bad people; they are misunderstood. Due to this hidden misunderstanding, they treat others how they unconsciously feel, think, or behave. For this reason, we must seek to understand the WHY of what we are doing, saying, or becoming. But more importantly, even if we do not fully understand our WHY or God has not unveiled it as of yet, at least we are fully aware of it. For sure, it helps to cut through the red tape of lies that we mend our secret wounds with.

Just so we are clear, we have all wrestled with how we should deal with something or someone in our heads, saying all types of things as our mental chatter chats away. While simultaneously experiencing all types of high and low emotions accompanying the mental pictures of giving someone a piece of our mind. However, fighting or warring with others in our imaginative thoughts does not necessarily make us a bully until it is manifested outwardly.

According to the Heavenly of Heavens, it is imperative to set a guard over the mind, ensuring our inner battles do not make it into reality, or we can counteract it with what is good, positive, productive, and fruitful.

What is the purpose of counteracting our negative thoughts, words, or emotions with positive fruits or character traits, *As It Pleases God*? It exemplifies our ability to self-correct or self-deflate using the Fruits of the Spirit while developing our people skills without having to play cleanup. What is the big deal? According to scripture: *"But I say to you that whoever is angry with his brother without a cause shall be in danger of the judgment. And whoever says to his brother, 'Raca!' (Empty Headed or Empty One) shall be in danger of the council. But whoever says, 'You fool!' shall be in danger of hell fire."* Matthew 5:22.

We cannot walk around insulting God, ourselves, and others just because we feel like it. Using derogatory statements to demean, provoke, or reject becomes a secret stairwell to the abyss, depending upon our motives and heart posture.

Regardless of what we are going through or the bullies we encounter along the way, we must hold steadfast to our faith. Listed below are a few things we must know and understand beyond a shadow of a doubt:

- ☐ *"Blessed are the poor in spirit, for theirs is the kingdom of heaven."* Matthew 5:3.
- ☐ *"Blessed are those who mourn, for they shall be comforted."* Matthew 5:4.
- ☐ *"Blessed are the meek, for they shall inherit the earth.* Matthew 5:5.
- ☐ *"Blessed are those who hunger and thirst for righteousness, for they shall be filled."* Matthew 5:6.
- ☐ *"Blessed are the merciful, for they shall obtain mercy."* Matthew 5:7.
- ☐ *"Blessed are the pure in heart, for they shall see God."* Matthew 5:8.
- ☐ *"Blessed are the peacemakers, for they shall be called sons of God."* Matthew 5:9.

- ☐ "Blessed are those who are persecuted for righteousness' sake, for theirs is the kingdom of heaven." Matthew 5:10.
- ☐ "Blessed are you when they revile and persecute you, and say all kinds of evil against you falsely for My sake." Matthew 5:11.
- ☐ "Rejoice and be exceedingly glad, for great is your reward in heaven, for so they persecuted the prophets who were before you." Matthew 5:12.
- ☐ "You are the salt of the earth; but if the salt loses its flavor, how shall it be seasoned? It is then good for nothing but to be thrown out and trampled underfoot by men." Matthew 5:13.
- ☐ "You are the light of the world. A city that is set on a hill cannot be hidden. Nor do they light a lamp and put it under a basket, but on a lampstand, and it gives light to all who are in the house. Let your light so shine before men, that they may see your good works and glorify your Father in heaven." Matthew 5:14-16.

When people attempt to throw us out to the wolves by developing their own technicalities to discredit us, we must apply the above Spiritual Principles. Doing so helps us to stay focused on the Will of God, not the will of man.

Getting to the top by crushing others will symbolically put a stain on our shoes, contaminating the building material of everywhere we place our feet until the intentional debauchery is repented. What does this mean? Our behavior is a SEED, bearing fruit in or out of Season. What is more, the same negative cycle will continue in our lives with different characters or in the lives of our loved ones. Really? Yes, really! According to scripture, *"For with what judgment you judge, you will be judged; and with the measure you use, it will be measured back to you."* Matthew 7:2.

How can we change our ways? The conditioned behaviors of bullying can be regrafted by using the Fruits of the Spirit without deviation and exhibiting Christlike Character in all our ways. What if we do not know what to do? Biblically, get into this mindset: *"Whatever you want men to do to you, do also to them, for this is the Law and the Prophets."* Matthew 7:12.

When we take the time to understand ourselves from the inside out, we will not exhibit a lot of negative behaviors due to the Spiritual Implications associated. In addition, we must also take into consideration adding a few elements to our daily lives. They are, but not limited to such:

- ☐ We need to exhibit *openness*.
- ☐ We must become *agreeable* to understanding without becoming outright disagreeably misunderstood.
- ☐ We must become *enthusiastic* about God, ourselves, and others.
- ☐ We must become *carefully thoughtful* in all things, deciphering right from wrong, good from evil, just from unjust, positive from negative, etc.
- ☐ We need to become *consistent* Mentally, Emotionally, Physically, and Spiritually to avoid the elements of distrust due to a wishy-washy demeanor.

We do not have to become a dry log in our approach to God, ourselves, or others. If we feel the bully rising from within, we should apply the above traits to influence our behavior toward a more positive outcome, *As It Pleases God*. If we do not interject positivity to break the negative, our influence can be perceived as unappealing or outright appalling.

The goal is to become positively receptive, kind, sociable, and conversational without being boisterous, unkind, rude, unapproachable, or dogmatic. Once again, those who are bullies do not realize that they are. Plus, they will become offended when their behavior is pointed out.

Most bullies are really sensitive, appearing strong, confident, and powerful. We must also understand that they are quick to seek revenge against those who call them out on their waywardness.

Just so we are clear, I am not pointing the finger; I am merely the Messenger sent from God to *Unveil the Veiled*.

Our positive or negative fixations of comfort or dis-ease from our past traumas, regrets, or pleasures set the tone of whether or not we become a bully or anti-bully. Still, ultimately, we make the final decision. Also, it determines whether we feel in or out of control of our lives as well.

Just keep in mind that no one is in 100% control or out of control of everything; it is an ILLUSION. In my opinion, this should fall under the 80/20 Rule, meaning 80% in control (self-control, thought-control, word-control, and emotional-control) and 20% in a work-in-progress status. Besides, if we were in control of everything, why would we need faith, right?

For me, I allow God to take the wheel of my life and bullies, *As It Pleases Him*, doing my part, Spiritually Tilling my own ground. With this Divine Mindset and according to my Predestined Blueprint, what is for me will be. And what is not for me will NOT be, as I keep it moving in the Spirit of Excellence, doing what I am called to do, using the Fruits of the Spirit, and behaving Christlike.

We are God's project for the Heaven on Earth experience, and the moment we forget our Divine Mission, we tend to repeat life lessons, becoming susceptible to a cycle of déjà vu, regardless of how powerful we think we are. By far, this keeps the inner bully from crushing us or those who are tipping the scales either way. God's way of measuring our potential and abilities is not man's way of doing so. He measures the heart posture along with our willingness, discipline, obedience, and trainability, *As It Pleases Him*.

On the other hand, when it comes down to our worldly system, we use another man's test or analysis process to determine the level of worthiness, intelligence, or aptitude of another, and sometimes rightfully so. Still, we cannot be 100% accurate. A man-made system is not 100% foolproof; therefore, it leaves room for error, improvement, or bullying.

With the Kingdom of Heaven, we play by different rules because we have the Holy Spirit to guide, correct, and teach us the Secrets of the Spirit, correcting the correctable. Is there an error in the

Spirit? No. The Spirit is Spiritually Absolute, similar to God being Absolute (Complete and Unchanging), because we are all the same.

If bullying makes its way to the physical realm, it means that we are in the flesh or we are engaging in some form of self-loathing. How can we break the desire to bully? To contend with our inner bully, we must unveil it with humility. It takes discipline to make our Body, Mind, and Soul behave. Really? Yes, really! If one does not believe this, remove something or someone the flesh likes; it will quickly make a believer out of us.

Unbeknown to most, in the Eye of God, the psyche is a bully, causing the warring of the SOUL and SPIRIT. Our carnal nature (the nature of the beast from within) conflicts with our Spiritual Nature. From the Garden of Eden until this very moment, the nature of the beast does not want to be tamed, *As It Pleases God*. How can we tame our human nature? We must become ONE with the Holy Trinity, we must forgive, and we must repent. In addition, we must also use the Word of God, the Fruits of the Spirit, and behave Christlike. Here is what we must know: *"For the word of God is living and powerful, and sharper than any two-edged sword, piercing even to the division of soul and spirit, and of joints and marrow, and is a discerner of the thoughts and intents of the heart."* Hebrews 4:12.

Now, to become a usable Vessel of the Kingdom, we must awaken our Spirit. According to the Heavenly of Heavens, this is how we humbly connect to the Holy Spirit and the Word of God, to chastise the lusts of the eye, the lusts of the flesh, and the pride of life, *As It Pleases God*.

Contrary to what most would think, humility does not mean we have low self-esteem, nor does it mean we lack confidence. True humility gives us the COURAGE to embrace our Spiritual Faith without proving ourselves to anyone but God Almighty. If we dare to exhibit the Fruits of the Spirit and Christlike Character when being humble, it gives us an inner freedom to become valuable in Earthen Vessels, impacting others on behalf of the Kingdom.

When we allow people to be who they are while becoming a light to illuminate Spiritual Growth without having to say one word, we are on the right path. How is this possible? We must become an EXAMPLE or a MIRROR for them. But more importantly, humility helps us to deal with those who appear difficult. Why does this work best? They do not feel like they have to fight with us or feel threatened to be who they are.

When we allow the Love and Word of God to pulsate through us into the lives of others, they can feel it, even if they pretend not to feel anything. Why do they pretend? They are really looking for consistency before they trust. Simply put, they are testing our Spirit, similar to how God tests us before commissioning us.

We are designed to bring the best out of the Kingdom, ourselves, and others. If we digress from this formality, we will find ourselves secretly or openly digging ditches for others to fall into while at the same time hiding our hands. But more importantly, behaving in such a manner, from a Spiritual Perspective, feeds the fallen state of the individuals who have not repented of this behavior. What is more, if we continue in this state, we will eventually dig our own ditch into which we or someone we love will fall; therefore, we must become cautious about our motives and our manipulative bullying tactics.

As Believers, we are called to a higher standard. God does not need bullies to boss around His sheep. He needs those who can Shepherd them without biases blocking their ability to hear His Voice, ushering His sheep in, out, and through the Spiritual Folds. We all need help at some point, and we do not want to become misled in our time of need. So, we should not do this to another.

In or out of our fallen or risen state of being, when we look back over our lives, what do we have to say about ourselves? What do we see? Or, better yet, what are we hearing? Why do we need to answer these questions? We have the power over our inner or outer bully when we know what we are saying, seeing, hearing, and becoming. If we do not know we have power over the bully, then we can become sifted due to our lack of understanding. Besides, without an understanding, we set ourselves up to become yoked, sifted, or justifiably veiled.

The moment we secretly or openly condemn ourselves, we set the stage to condemn the Kingdom and others. If our bullying tactics have manifested physically, we must remember that it takes a bully to bully. According to our DNA construct, we must bully ourselves first, before the manifestation of how we treat ourselves inwardly makes its way outwardly.

Bullies knowingly or unknowingly ingest toxins and spew them out without realizing their implications from a Spiritual Perspective. Unfortunately, bullies are dealing with the hidden elements of jealousy, envy, pride, greed, ungratefulness, covetousness, and rebellion boiling over within the depths of their souls. In light of this, we must be very cautious about being out of the Will of God, outright rejecting Him, or not trying to become righteous at all. Without such caution, we are left to ourselves to figure things out through our worldly lenses instead of our Spiritual Ones.

If we find ourselves fighting against God, we will discover that we are really fighting against ourselves from the inside out. Our internal '*fight or flight*' response, designed to save our lives, becomes stuck in the '*fight*' mode when we bully without correcting our behavior. Unfortunately, this is often recognized when we are always defensive about everything, easily triggered, or have an excuse for misbehaving.

In the country, we call this hormonal response the '*Mother Hen*' or '*Father Rooster*' Complex. By far, this is when we know we, our spouse, or our children are doing wrong. Still, we are ready to fight anyway instead of apologizing, assuming responsibility, making the necessary corrections, or exhibiting outright humility. In addition, this also happens when we think everyone is out to hurt, use, abuse, or traumatize us. Oddly, we will find bullies threatening others, but we must also consider that they feel threatened as well. How do we know when we are threatened or if someone feels threatened by us? Usually, it is recognized in a few ways, but not limited to such:

- ☐ Whining to manipulate is an indicator.
- ☐ Fussing, ranting, and raving about everything to control it, them, or that are indicators.
- ☐ Fighting to prove strength is an indicator.

- ☐ Being on the attack or confrontational without provocation is an indicator.
- ☐ Exploding with emotions of sarcasm or foolery is an indicator.
- ☐ Imploding with rage, rudeness, hatefulness, or negativity is an indicator.
- ☐ Breaking bonds by the inability to keep promises or tell the truth is an indicator.
- ☐ Frustrated by life, snapping, or cutting a person's head off is an indicator.
- ☐ Avoiding being corrected or passing the blame is an indicator.
- ☐ Looking for the bad while overlooking the good is an indicator.
- ☐ When we overcommit, causing us to under-deliver on a promise is an indicator.
- ☐ Having a thwarted perception and seeking any attention are indicators.

God is not out of date; He is alive and active, seeking to fulfill His Divine Covenant to weed out the undercover bullies. Regardless of whether our intentions are good or not, it behooves us to learn how to communicate effectively, be kind to those who despitefully use us, help those who are not helpful, love those who are hateful, and the list goes on. Why should we go out of our way to do good in such a manner? First and foremost, we are not perfect, and we all need a checkup from the neck up on occasion. Secondly, it helps to build character positively without being an egotistical 'Know-It-All' or a negative 'Catch-All.' Thirdly, it helps us to become clear about our motives, developing consistency as opposed to wishy-washiness, knowing when to say 'Yes' or 'No' and mean it, without wavering.

We are designed to inspire those around us, sparking a desire for others to become better on their own accord or to make positive changes for the better without bullying them, causing them to shut down or shut us out. But more importantly, if we have a desire to build our Repertoire of Greatness, we must master the ability to help others by learning their language without speaking down to them or degrading their intelligence. How is this possible when a bully is right in front of us? Kindness is key! From my perspective, if we master the ability to be kind to ourselves, it becomes easier to extend it to others.

We are all entitled to our own opinions, and just because a person's opinion and views differ, it does not mean we should not exhibit the Fruits of the Spirit or Christlike Character. By Divine Design, God intended for us to be effectively fruitful, consistent, proactive, righteous, and appreciative. Although our personalities vary from person to person, it does not mean that we should become indifferent. However, when we feel out of control, our differences may become apparent, but it should not cause us to become biased, cruel, impatient, or manipulative.

Everyone has a journey, and we all exist for a reason. We cannot walk around consciously oblivious to someone who is hurting or someone who needs our help. Nor can we judge someone by material gain; we must find a way to look beyond the physical or worldly means of judging God's sheep.

According to the Heavenly of Heavens, God will always place our BLESSINGS in people, places, and things we would presumably reject. For many, it is designed to test our Spiritual Discernment, Fruits, and HEART POSTURE. Besides, we will never know when the tables will turn in our favor or away from it, or whether we are the stepping stone for the Divine Cornerstone.

For example, we have nine broke people, and we invest the Fruits of the Spirit and Christlike Character into their lives without rejecting them...not only do we become BLESSED, the nine also become BLESSED as well. Here is what Matthew 25:40 advises: *"And the King will answer and say to them, Assuredly, I say to you, inasmuch as you did it to one of the least of these My brethren, you did it to Me."*

If we refuse to share the Fruits of the Spirit or Christlike Character when it is within our power to do so, it creates inner depletion from the soulish realm. How is this possible when we have the free will to do whatever we like or help whomever? We all have a responsibility to do our part in whatever God has ordained for us to do, learn, or share. Here is what Colossians 3:23-25 says to us: *"And whatever you do, do it heartily, as to the Lord and not to men, knowing that from the Lord you will receive the reward of the inheritance; for you serve the Lord Christ. But he who does wrong will be repaid for what he has done, and there is no partiality."*

Listen, regardless of where we are in life or what type of bully we have become, the Fruits of the Spirit and Christlike Character change lives, period! Let me take this a step further: we all know the story of the Good Samaritan, right? If not, it is a good read located in Luke 10:25-37. However, let me go over it, *"A certain man went down from Jerusalem to Jericho, and fell among thieves, who stripped him of his clothing, wounded him, and departed, leaving him half dead. Now by chance a certain priest came down that road. And when he saw him, he passed by on the other side. Likewise a Levite, when he arrived at the place, came and looked, and passed by on the other side. But a certain Samaritan, as he journeyed, came where he was. And when he saw him, he had compassion. So he went to him and bandaged his wounds, pouring on oil and wine; and he set him on his own animal, brought him to an inn, and took care of him. On the next day, when he departed, he took out two denarii, gave them to the innkeeper, and said to him, 'Take care of him; and whatever more you spend, when I come again, I will repay you.' So which of these three do you think was neighbor to him who fell among the thieves? And he said, 'He who showed mercy on him.' Then Jesus said to him, Go and do likewise."* Is this not why we are in the predicament we are in today? Absolutely!

We have nine rich people who invested in us without leading us back to our Creator, and they do not teach the power of pulling up another; then what do we have? An unprofitable servant. If we willfully choose to have a hole in our soul to fill our pockets, something is definitely wrong somewhere, especially when we have the option of filling both if we follow proper Spiritual Protocol. *"For what will it profit a man if he gains the whole world, and loses his own soul?"* Mark 8:36. Without being in Purpose on purpose or not using our Gifts, Creativity, and Talents, we can easily become misled by worldly means, which will cause us to come back searching for God anyway.

If we only hang with people for what they can do for us, unfortunately, we have God all wrong! Listen, and listen to me well; we are BLESSED to be a BLESSING. This Heaven on Earth experience is about what we can do for God and others while availing ourselves as a Spiritual Vessel. For the ultimate experience in life, we must do what we were called to do without falling in love with the wrong things. Here is what 1 John 2:15 tells us: *"Do not love the world or the things in the world. If anyone loves the world, the love of the Father is not in him."*

We did not enter this world by ourselves; we needed help getting here, right? If we think that we are above helping another innocent life, then we are sadly mistaken. Truthfully, regardless of anyone's past mistakes, dilemmas, or mishaps, we are not different from needing help ourselves. Plus, if we unveil our real story, we will find the same mistakes, dilemmas, or mishaps filed under a different label. Some we got caught, exposed, or chastised for; yet, there are still some things God has veiled. What is more, we all have strengths and weaknesses; therefore, we should never turn up our noses at someone. We never know who that person is, who they may become, or how God may use the situation, circumstance, or event to benefit the Kingdom of Heaven.

We may not be able to save the world, but we can definitely do our part. When God places someone in our circle, we cannot become like Jonah, overlooking or running from the Mission of God. If we somehow get offended, we must learn how to reverse negatives into positives, shake it off, and keep it moving without looking down on another. Furthermore, everyone crosses our path for a reason, season, lesson, or lifetime. If we are not becoming a living example for them to mirror, then we need to step back into the Spiritual Classroom to master a few Biblical Principles.

- ☐ *"The truth is in Jesus."* Ephesians 4:21b.
- ☐ *"That you put off, concerning your former conduct, the old man which grows corrupt according to the deceitful lusts."* Ephesians 4:22.

- ☐ *"Be renewed in the spirit of your Mind."* Ephesians 4:23.
- ☐ *"Put on the new man which was created according to God, in true righteousness and holiness."* Ephesians 4:24.
- ☐ *"Therefore, putting away lying, 'Let each one of you speak truth with his neighbor,' for we are members of one another."* Ephesians 4:25.
- ☐ *"Be angry, and do not sin: do not let the sun go down on your wrath."* Ephesians 4:26.
- ☐ *"Do not give place to the devil."* Ephesians 4:27.
- ☐ *"Let him who stole steal no longer, but rather let him labor, working with his hands what is good, that he may have something to give him who has need."* Ephesians 4:28.
- ☐ *"Let no corrupt word proceed out of your mouth, but what is good for necessary edification, that it may impart grace to the hearers."* Ephesians 4:29.
- ☐ *"And do not grieve the Holy Spirit of God, by whom you were sealed for the day of redemption."* Ephesians 4:30.
- ☐ *"Let all bitterness, wrath, anger, clamor, and evil speaking be put away from you, with all malice."* Ephesians 4:31.
- ☐ *"Be kind to one another, tenderhearted, forgiving one another, even as God in Christ forgave you."* Ephesians 4:32.

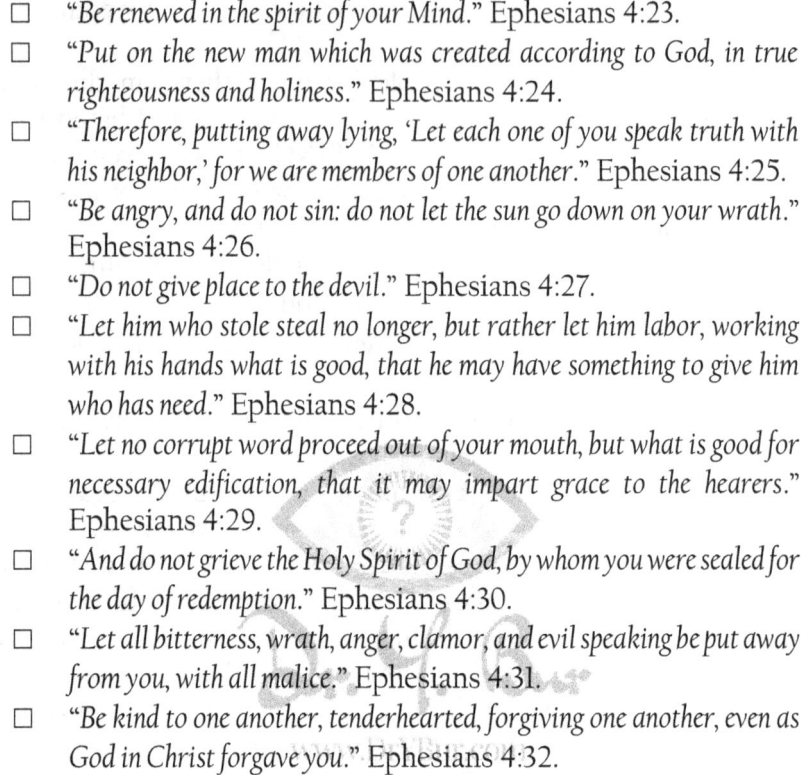

We need to AWAKEN ourselves to the newness of the *Silent Whispers* of the Kingdom. Here is what we must know, *As It Pleases God:* "Do not lie to one another, since you have put off the old man with his deeds, and have put on the new man who is renewed in knowledge according to the image of Him who created him, where there is neither Greek nor Jew, circumcised nor uncircumcised, barbarian, Scythian, slave nor free, but Christ is all and in all. Therefore, as the elect of God, holy and beloved, put on tender mercies, kindness, humility, meekness, longsuffering; bearing with one another, and forgiving one another, if anyone has a complaint against another; even as Christ forgave you, so you also must do. But above all these things put on love, which is the bond of perfection. And let the peace of God rule in your hearts, to which also you were called in one body; and be thankful." Colossians 3:9-15.

Chapter 10

SILENT WHISPERS

We often think of *Whispers* as being the audibly monotone spoken voice. However, from my perspective, the secret is hidden in the SILENCE. Yet the profound, inaudible voice of the Great Unknown is from within the human psyche, possessing the ability to communicate *Spirit to Spirit* with our Heavenly Father. The moment we dare to step outside of our environmental conditioning into Spiritual Training, we avail ourselves to reach beyond our self-imposed limitations to embrace what is coveted by those without a Divine Connection, *As It Pleases God*.

Unbeknown to most, the *Silent Whispers* cannot receive the appropriate Spiritual Reception if our wires are secretly, unawaringly, or openly crossed. For this reason, on behalf of the Heavenly of Heavens, we are ripping the Spiritual Veil, getting to the nitty-gritty of the wiles of the enemy.

From the Garden of Eden, the enemy has invoked a siege of misunderstanding, miscommunication, misrepresentation, misbehaving, aloofness, or disrespectfulness against the Kingdom. How is this possible, especially since that was back then and this is now? Simply put, this tactic is used when we think we are hearing the Voice of God, but it is the voice of the enemy speaking due to our lack of inner peace, negativity, doubtfulness, insecurities, or Spiritual Unrest. Unfortunately, this was used on Eve, then she used it on Adam, and then He tried to use it on God Almighty. Therefore, the dominoes will not stop falling until we

Spiritually Seal this, *As It Pleases God*, doing our due diligence and Spiritually Tilling our own ground.

The *Silent Whispers* of yesterday, today, and forever speak to those who have a willing ear to hear, but we must also have selective listening to ensure we hear correctly and discern properly as well. Everything we hear, do, become, or say is NOT always of God, regardless of how we feel, believe, or think. So, it is imperative to align our '*Silent Whispers*' with scripture to ensure we do not become misled by our hidden lusts or biased conditionings. How do we know the difference? We can determine the difference in two ways:

- ☐ By the Fruits of the Spirit with selfless encouragement toward righteousness.

- ☐ By the fruits of deception toward selfishness and unrighteousness.

Often enough, I have those who proclaim not to have any lust at all; however, let me make this statement right now before we go any further: We all will deal with lust, period! The difference is that some are controlled, and some are not. Yet, they are usually hidden underneath what we consider as habits. One may sound a little more palatable than the other, but in the Eye of God, they are the same.

If we pinpoint our habits, we can usually unveil the category of our lusts. Is this Biblical? Of course, *"For all that is in the world—the lust of the flesh, the lust of the eyes, and the pride of life—is not of the Father but is of the world. And the world is passing away, and the lust of it; but he who does the will of God abides forever."* 1 John 2:16-17.

The *Silent Whispers* of our lusts are nothing to be afraid of unless we act upon them. As a part of our humanness, thoughts come and go, but we have the power to give in or cast down our thoughts. Really? Yes, really. Let us take it to scripture; it says, *"I say then: Walk in the Spirit, and you shall not fulfill the lust of the flesh. For the flesh lusts* against the Spirit, and the Spirit against the flesh; and these are contrary to one another, so that you do not do the things that you wish. But if you are led by the Spirit, you are not under the law." Galatians 5:16-18. If we are misbehaving without repentance or correction, it is not the Spirit of God leading. Then who is leading us? The flesh!

In today's time, if we cast down vain imaginations, we would call this self-correction, self-control, or self-conviction, especially if we are in control of ourselves with the Holy Spirit's help. On the other hand, if we give in to vain imaginations or have unrestrained lusts, it is often referred to as unconvicted, undisciplined, reckless, or conscienceless. By far, this is where we ignore correction as it becomes our normal due to NOT having the Holy Trinity involved.

How do we know if we are engaging in the lust of the flesh? According to scripture, it says, "Now the works of the flesh are evident, which are: adultery, fornication, uncleanness, lewdness, idolatry, sorcery, hatred, contentions, jealousies, outbursts of wrath, selfish ambitions, dissensions, heresies, envy, murders, drunkenness, revelries, and the like; of which I tell you beforehand, just as I also told you in time past, that those who practice such things will not inherit the Kingdom of God." Galatians 5:19-21.

Can we function in the Kingdom in such a manner? Absolutely. God will not violate our free will to do, say, think, and become whatever we like. This is blasphemy, right? Wrong! We all have issues to work on or work at in the midst of doing the Will of God. The key is to understand the weakness, repent, forgive, and honestly work on doing better, learn the lesson, and understand the Spiritual Principles to BENEFIT the Kingdom of God with a work-in-progress mentality. By no means am I perfect; it is through my imperfections that I come back to TEACH these Spiritual Principles with clean hands and a pure heart, *As It Pleases God*.

In the Kingdom, experience makes the BEST Spiritual Teachers. Using the Fruits of the Spirit makes them BETTER Teachers, and exhibiting Christlike Character makes them GREAT in the Eye of God. What makes them the best, better, and great, *As It Pleases God*? We have compassion, patience, commitment, understanding, and MERCY in areas that most people nitpick, reject, offend, and judge due to their lack of experience and Spiritual Training from the Heavenly of Heavens.

Now, on the other hand, if our folly in the Kingdom is left uncorrected or unrepentant, we become accountable for every individual we have misled, especially if any form of deception is involved. In my opinion, it is like a DOUBLE-EDGED SWORD if we play with God in such a manner. Why does it come back double? The Spiritual Penalty is higher when we know better while choosing not to do better, hurting innocent people who are making their best attempts to heal.

How can we make our best attempts when we are struggling in a few areas? The best antidote for any form of struggle is to repent, forgive, and wholeheartedly use the Fruits of the Spirit. Where is this in the Bible? Galatians 5:22-23 says, *"But the fruit of the Spirit is love, joy, peace, longsuffering (patience), kindness, goodness, faithfulness, gentleness, and self-control. Against such there is no law."* This is our Secret Weapon of Warfare to combat or understand the *Silent Whispers* from God, ourselves, others, or the enemy, enabling us to know the difference.

When we hear a silent voice, we must TEST the Spirit by aligning it with the Fruits of the Spirit. What is the best way of doing so? Here is how I do it by asking:

- ☐ Is it exhibiting Love?
- ☐ Is it exhibiting Joy?
- ☐ Is it exhibiting Peace?
- ☐ Is it exhibiting Patience?
- ☐ Is it exhibiting Kindness?
- ☐ Is it exhibiting Goodness?
- ☐ Is it exhibiting Faithfulness?
- ☐ Is it exhibiting Gentleness?
- ☐ Is it exhibiting Self-Control?

If the answer is 'No,' it is not the Holy Spirit; it is self, the enemy from within, or the enemy of deception speaking. How can we possibly test what is Holy? Let us take it to scripture to ensure we understand Spiritual Protocol. It says, "*Beloved, do not believe every spirit, but test the spirits, whether they are of God; because many false prophets have gone out into the world.*" 1 John 4:1.

In or out of our fleshly desires, wants, and know-how, when conflict occurs Mentally, Physically, Emotionally, or Spiritually, we have the option to deal with it, redirect it, or run from it. If we do not have all the information, we cannot effectively draw a precise conclusion, right? Therefore, we must learn how to ask fact-finding questions without offending, prying, or intruding by becoming crystal-clear about our intentions.

Suppose a level of trust is not obtained. In this case, the value in our level of communication suffers on the speaker's and listener's behalf, giving The *Silent Whispers* free rein to do whatever, whenever, however, wherever, and with whomever. How is this possible? We are all different with our very own way of perceiving what is being said, heard, and learned; therefore, the mind can create whatever it desires to justify the psyche's analysis, positively or negatively. At the same time, it involves selective listening, understanding, comprehending, and salutations, determining our people skills and the lack thereof.

For example, if I am speaking one way based on my perceived knowledge and understanding, the hearer may interpret it another way based on theirs; therefore, both lenses of communication must be clear. What is the big deal about perceiving and hearing? If we want our heart's desires or embark upon our Divine Destiny, we must clear the way for it through our ability to perceive and hear correctly while relating accordingly. Nonetheless, do not take my word for it; here is what the scriptures have to say, "*And He said, Go, and tell this people: Keep on hearing, but do not understand; keep on seeing, but do not perceive. Make the heart of this people dull, and their ears heavy, and shut their eyes; lest they see with their eyes, and hear with their ears, and understand with their heart, and return and be healed.*" Isaiah 6:9-10.

On the other side of The *Silent Whispers*, it wants us to know that our communication waves have a profound effect on us. How is this possible? We hear in vibrations, similar to animals. This is why we are moved positively or negatively by certain music, sounds, or tones. In addition, this is how we can tell if we heard something from the right, left, top, bottom, etc. Although this unique quality is taken for granted in the natural realm; yet, it is needed in the Spiritual. Why? It is connected to our Spiritual Instincts while helping us develop a soft approach to God, ourselves, and others.

Spiritually Speaking, if we are not in tune, *As It Pleases God*, we will miss the Holy Spirit's leading due to the misdirection or misunderstanding of our senses, conscience, and discernment. Doing so will cause us to approach people and the things of the Spirit amiss or outright miss our Spiritual Cue. Unfortunately, this is why we find ourselves saying a few statements, but not limited to such:

- ☐ Something told me not to do that.
- ☐ Something told me not to say that.
- ☐ Something told me I should not have gone there.
- ☐ Something told me they were not right for me.
- ☐ Something told me they were going to do this.
- ☐ Something told me I was going to get in trouble if I did that.
- ☐ Something told me I should have gone another way.
- ☐ Something told me to ask the question differently.
- ☐ Something told me that they were right for me.
- ☐ Something told me to say this.
- ☐ Something told me to look there.
- ☐ Something told me I was going to receive this.

The '*Something Told Me*' statements have been around since the Garden of Eden, and now we have to determine if the '*Something*' is coming from a good or evil place. What does this mean? Just as Eve was deceived in the Garden, we will become deceived in the world we live in today; so, we must stay on our toes to ensure we do not have another '*Adam and Eve Experience.*'

What is the '*Adam and Eve Experience?*' This experience is when we listen to the voices of another kind that disrupts our Divine

Purpose of being fruitful, multiplying, and replenishing the earth. Of course, this is not just about having babies or producing offspring. Spiritually, it is about giving life to another for the betterment of the Kingdom of Heaven for such a time as this.

How can we give life to another outside of our own? The Kingdom is a building process of birthing, giving life to people, places, things, ideas, creativity, etc. But more importantly, in the Kingdom process, some things must come down as well. What does this mean? As harsh as it seems, things die to provide life for another. Things like what? Listed below are a few items, but not limited to such:

- ☐ Our negative thoughts, words, actions, emotions, and desires must go.
- ☐ Our pompousness must go.
- ☐ Our ungratefulness must go.
- ☐ Our disobedience, stiff neck, and dullness must go.
- ☐ Our blindness, deafness, and muteness must go.
- ☐ Our loud mouth and loose lips must go.
- ☐ Our psychological mind games must go.
- ☐ Our lies and deceit must go.
- ☐ Our hatefulness and abusiveness must go.
- ☐ Our resistance and hatefulness must go.
- ☐ Our closed-mindedness or unforgiveness must go.
- ☐ Our jealousy, envy, strife, greed, and coveting must go.

Our '*Adam and Eve Experience*' can make us positively irresistible in the Kingdom if we learn how to go right where they went wrong, forcing the *Silent Whispers* to work on our behalf and not against us. How is this possible? We have to flip the script, get rid of the items listed above for starters, and then move on to align our lives with what God has in mind as it relates to the Kingdom of Heaven.

If we learn the Language of God, *As It Pleases Him*, He will perfect our Spiritual Language for our Heaven on Earth experiences automatically. Conversely, if we choose to please ourselves, the mental chatter will chat on, creating all types of unpleasant experiences, sifting our perception, or outright snatching our Gifting, Calling, Creativity, and Talents right before our very eyes. Why can we not see it? We are veiled. Simply put, we are Spiritually Blind, Deaf, and Mute to experience what is hidden in plain sight.

Does our Spiritual Language really matter when *Unveiling the Veiled*? Absolutely! When filtering the *Silent Whispers*, if we do not filter out the negative or unrighteousness, we can become hidden grenades without knowing it. As a result, we may have a meltdown coming out of nowhere. Then again, we may blow up or implode when the inner chatter is going a mile a minute, creating total unrest within the psyche.

Listen, regardless of what has become customary, loud, fast, or abusive talking disrupts the human psyche. But more importantly, even if we have become accustomed to this type of communication, our souls are taking notes, keeping a file of everything. Meanwhile, gentle, calm, and satiating speaking calms the psyche, even if we are hellions on wheels. Our language has enough power to fight or make peace, but we have to choose our intentions before setting our words in motion or allowing our thoughts to have free rein.

In the Beginning, we were designed to be at peace with ourselves, others, and our environment. And now, we must dig a little deeper to accomplish such a task. Why is this considered a task? It takes work to obtain, maintain, and sustain our level of peace. What is the purpose of knowing this? We are all subject to worldly disruptions such as anger, hurt, disappointment, grief, trauma, and so on. But let us align how we should respond to this: "*For His anger is but for a moment, His favor is for life; weeping may endure for a night, but joy comes in the morning.*" Psalm 30:5.

Our counterattack to any form of negative disposition is to use the Word of God as our ammunition. Regardless of what we are going through, have become involved in, or how many mistakes we have made, God's favor and forgiveness are renewed daily, letting bygones be bygones, *As It Pleases Him*.

God's way of dealing with issues is totally different from man's way of doing things. For example, we hold grudges when we think we have been wronged. Yet, in all truth, our wrongness is a matter of perception or a violation of another person's free will.

Most often, when someone exercises their free will in saying 'No' to us, we get upset, offended, or begrudged because we wanted a 'Yes.' Is this Godly behavior? No, it is selfish behavior. As hard as it may seem at times, this is why we need to do a checkup from the neck up periodically and fine-tune our opportunistic motives.

The human psyche is very fickle; it can get a thousand 'Yeses,' and the one time it gets a 'No,' it has the nerve to get upset, offended, vexed, or seek revenge, which is totally out of character for the Kingdom.

The *Silent Whispers* of negativity or evil can easily spring up within the depths of our souls, especially if we do not apply the Spiritual Principles of not violating the will of another. Is this Biblical? Absolutely. Matthew 5:37 says, *"But let your 'Yes' be 'Yes,' and your 'No,' be 'No.' For whatever is more than these is from the evil one."*

Every morning gives us a new opportunity to bask in God's Divine Blessings to understand the *Silent Whispers* of our Daily Bread. According to the Ancient of Days, it is our Divine Birthright to have our unrighteousness PASS OVER us, especially if we follow the proper Spiritual Protocols of doing so, *As It Pleases God*.

What does Pass Over have to do with us? In the Eye of God, it has everything to do with us, primarily if we use the Blood of Jesus as our Spiritual Atonement to ENFORCE the Everlasting Ordinance. Can we do this? Absolutely! Here is the Spiritual Seal for the Everlasting Ordinance: *"Now the blood shall be a sign for you on the houses where you are. And when I see the blood, I will pass over you; and the plague shall not be on you to destroy you when I strike the land of Egypt. So this day shall be to you a memorial; and you shall keep it as a feast to the LORD throughout your generations. You shall keep it as a feast by an everlasting ordinance."* Exodus 12:13-14.

In our *Spirit to Spirit* Relations with our Heavenly Father, He wants us to know: *"If we confess our sins, He is faithful and just to forgive us our sins and to cleanse us from all unrighteousness."* 1 John 1:9. What if we keep messing up? Rinse and repeat this process with a work-in-progress mentality, using the Fruits of the Spirit, and behave Christlike.

I cannot tell you how many times I messed up royally, but I got back on track, and now here we are. More importantly, my Divine Blueprint is now the Divinely Appointed unleavened bread with a trail of Spiritual Crumbs sustaining you. What does this mean? I will not feed you fluff and stuff. I come straight out of the gate with the Word of God, leading you back to the Kingdom, *As It Pleases Him*, allowing the Holy Spirit to do what He does best. All you need to do is give the Holy Spirit authorization to lead while covering yourself with the Blood of Jesus amid your mess.

Most often, our mess is usually a stepping stone designed to train, mold, and regraft us. How do we get unrighteousness to pass over our lives daily? It is wrapped in our acceptance, repentance, and faith with the covering of the Blood of Jesus. Is this Biblical? I would have it no other way, *"But now the righteousness of God apart from the law is revealed, being witnessed by the Law and the Prophets, even the righteousness of God, through faith in Jesus Christ, to all and on all who believe. For there is no difference; for all have sinned and fall short of the glory of God, being justified freely by His grace through the redemption that is in Christ Jesus, whom God set forth as a propitiation by His blood, through faith, to demonstrate His righteousness, because in His forbearance God had passed over the sins that were previously committed, to demonstrate at the present time His righteousness, that He might be just and the justifier of the one who has faith in Jesus."* Romans 3:21-26.

If we do not look for the good and positive outcomes in life, the *Silent Whispers* of the enemy can come in to provoke us, steal our peace, or get into our heads. For example, a passerby with a stick in her hand asked a friend of mine for $2. Out of the fear of what she was going to do with the stick, he opted not to risk opening his wallet in public. So, he responded, 'I do not have cash; I only have my debit card.' The woman knew he was lying because she was informed by the *Silent Whispers* of someone else before asking.

Unbeknownst, the seemingly trusted someone who gets a few dollars from my friend at times was a shuckster (a deceiver) who secretly pimped out his shickster (street walker) by advising her that he keeps plenty of cash on hand.

Now, due to her feelings of rejection and her outraged anger, she yelled out a racial slur to provoke him negatively. Instead, he kept crossing the road without responding to her, even though he was boiling over from within.

Why did he get so angry? He really wanted to help her out of the goodness of his heart. But the *Silent Whispers* from within advised him otherwise; therefore, he exhibited extreme caution.

But more importantly, on the other hand, the *Silent Whispers* from within can speak to insult, abuse, or manipulate to zap someone's positivity, peace, or happiness to make others feel likewise. Is this fair? Of course not, but this woman felt justified in making her best attempt to ruin this man's day for the $2 that he worked hard for.

What is the big deal behind $2? The deal is that she did not need the $2; she attempted to take advantage of the man by soliciting him with undercover prostitution. From her perspective, pedaling for a few dollars is not as bold or obvious as outright selling herself. So, with her self-aggrandizing business, she works best by striking up a conversation over $2, hoping the gentleman would ask for more, especially when he is capable of paying!

When it is all said and done, another side of the *Silent Whispers* can protect, forewarn, and expose the contents of the heart of another, causing us to exercise caution without realizing why we are doing so until after the fact. How do we make this make sense? The *Silent Whispers* from within caused his instincts to focus on the outcome as it relates to the stick she was carrying in her hand, as opposed to the true intent of this woman until she got out of character, yelping out a racial slur.

For this gentleman to vent correctly, he had to make peace with how blessed he was. How did he come to terms with his blessings? First, he understood the importance of not being the one asking for $2. Secondly, he recognized the true blessing of having a job to finance his lifestyle. Thirdly, he realized his God-Given opportunity of having free will to create a win-win, preventing the *Silent Whispers* of negativity from stealing his joy or getting into his head, causing him to have a bad day. As a result, he went back to work with a smile on his face, making the most of his ability to reverse a negative into a positive at the drop of a dime.

The power of our Testimony can change lives for the better, especially if we learn how to create a win-win. Had my friend not shared the *Silent Whispers* of this story with me, I would not be able to share it with another, allowing God to get the glory out of this.

Chapter 11

THE SPIRITUAL SENSATION

In and out of the world we live in today, if we look around and pay close attention, we will notice the people, places, and things we did not see previously, especially if we take the time to hone in with our senses. As it relates to becoming a *Spiritual Sensation*, we cannot fail to pay attention or become distracted by what we perceive as important and what is not. For this reason alone, it behooves us to tap into our senses from a Spiritual Perspective to maximize our full potential for this Heaven on Earth Experience, *As It Pleases God*.

Just so we are clear, when *Unveiling the Veiled*, what catches our attention is neither right nor wrong; it is merely a matter of our free will choice in need of sensible filtering. However, when it comes down to our Spiritual Senses, we are called to pay attention while staying at full alert, even when we are asleep. How is this possible? Unbeknown to most, we have the power to command our Spirit to stand at full alert when we are asleep. Really? Yes, really!

Contrary to what most think, our Spirit does not sleep when it has been Spiritually Awakened. Our Body, Mind, and Soul will need rest. Meanwhile, our Spirit does not, once it is Awakened.

If we do not make a conscious choice to become ONE with the Holy Spirit, it will not violate our free will. Our Spirit will remain in a dormant state until we have made a conscious decision to demand its presence. As a result of this form of Spiritual Dormancy, we will find ourselves Spiritually Blind, Deaf, and Mute to the Elements of the Great Unknown until we come to ourselves.

Due to this known or unknown Spiritual Paralysis, we must also understand that once our Spirit becomes ONE with the Holy Spirit, it transforms into a Spiritual Absolute as long as we are willing. The moment this Spiritual Union is made, it is bound by Spiritual Laws governing a non-violation zone of free will. While simultaneously having our best interest at heart to guide, correct, teach, and protect us for our Heaven on Earth Experience, *As It Pleases God*, and according to our Predestined Blueprint.

How do we Spiritually Awaken ourselves from our slumber? From a Spiritual Perspective, we must tune into our human senses to alter our perceptions. Our senses and perceptions are cousin-like in the Spirit, making them distantly related, but definitely related indeed. What does this mean? It simply means that our senses may not directly impact us in our present state of being. However, down the line, if left unguarded, the impact will create a *VEIL* without us realizing it is there.

According to the Heavenly of Heavens, *The Spiritual Sensation* we need is wrapped in how we respond to a few things, but not limited to such:

- ☐ Light.
- ☐ Darkness.
- ☐ Sounds.
- ☐ Odors.
- ☐ Vibrations.
- ☐ Textures.
- ☐ Tastes.
- ☐ Movements.
- ☐ Love.
- ☐ Hate.
- ☐ Blessings.
- ☐ Curses.

Most often, we would not associate blessings and curses or love and hate with our senses. But if the truth is told, our Soul feels or recognizes them all, determining how we perceive the people, places, and things we come in contact with. How is this possible? They are all energy, and so are we! It takes energy to create energy, right? Absolutely! So, the energy comprised in our senses is profoundly real, taking us positively to the next level, bringing us down beneath our level, or manifesting the inner chatter of negativity.

But more importantly, God has designed the largest sensory organ (the skin) to cover or hold the smaller sensory items such as the eyes, ears, mouth, tongue, and nose. They all send signals to the Mind, Body, Soul, and Spirit to keep us balanced.

Now, if our Spirit is asleep, then we have the Mind, Body, and Soul to work with, creating a known or unknown imbalance within the three. If our Mind is asleep (consumed with negative or evil chatter), we have only the Body and Soul to maneuver. Unfortunately, this is where our conscience becomes worldly without any form of Spiritual Reckoning, allowing our Mind to become controlled by anything or anyone. Is this real? Absolutely!

If we cannot calculate Godliness into the equation of our everyday living, we can easily be sifted. Why can we be easily sifted when God is the Lord over our lives and the Blood of Jesus covers us? Whether we are Believers or not, when our perception is off, our impulses will not transmit the proper signals. We will not be able to convert negatives into positives, see the light in the darkness, or properly process life pressures from the inside out. More so, if we continue in this manner without finding a way to *Unveil* ourselves, we will become Spiritually Impaired due to our worldliness and inner hallucinations, where our thoughts become inaccurate with self-induced untruths.

What do self-induced untruths have to do with our *Spiritual Sensations*? Most of the issues or traumas we are wrestling with are created by us, through us, and for us. What does this mean? Our issues or traumas are self-created in a few ways:

- ☐ By the way we think and speak.
- ☐ By the way we perceive and communicate.
- ☐ Our inability to forgive and repent.

- ☐ By misunderstanding the intent.
- ☐ By not being able to convert a negative into a positive.
- ☐ By not being able to create a win-win situation.
- ☐ By not being able to ask the right fact-finding questions.
- ☐ By not getting an understanding or being selfish.
- ☐ By violating the free will of another.
- ☐ By developing a deaf ear due to our biases or conditioning.
- ☐ By becoming defiant or rude, exhibiting ungodly behaviors or responses.
- ☐ By not aligning our lives or the situation with Biblical Scriptures or Principles, *As It Pleases God*.

How we perceive God, ourselves, others, and life determines our reality. Be it natural or Spiritual, our senses take notes and decide on, file, organize, and allocate the information sent to the psyche. Then, the soulish psyche decides what is queued to mentally replay unless we train it to process and perceive properly or Godly. Is this possible to do? Absolutely! We have free will to put the proper restraints in place, or we can allow it to run free, creating all types of illusions for us to partake in, adapt, or respond to through a few means, but not limited to such:

- ☐ Selective Seeing.
- ☐ Selective Hearing.
- ☐ Selective Tasting.
- ☐ Selective Smelling.
- ☐ Selective Feelings.
- ☐ Selective Touching.
- ☐ Selective Attention.
- ☐ Selective Consciousness.
- ☐ Selective Conditioning.
- ☐ Selective Thinking.
- ☐ Selective Actions.
- ☐ Selective Provocations.

Believe it or not, we are experts in this filtering process. It is hidden in our ability to ignore, reject, or overlook people, places, and things based on our feelings, traumas, biases, conditioning, hatefulness, or unforgiveness.

We all can accept or reject anything or anyone Mentally, Physically, Emotionally, and Spiritually at the drop of a dime. Most often, we exercise this privilege subconsciously, working against us negatively. How? Simply put, we do not know what we are doing or why, allowing this process to be on autopilot with the 'whatever goes' or 'going with the flow' mentality. However, when we become consciously mindful of this perceptional process, we can become a *Spiritual Sensation*, especially when we can pinpoint or diagnose our thoughts, actions, words, emotions, triggers, nudges, or memories and govern them accordingly, *As It Pleases God*.

Being able to reel ourselves in from the inside out gives us Spiritual Leverage to repent and forgive quickly. Why is this necessary? We can become truthful about the point of origin or the root cause of an issue. Either way, owning our truth creates a platform for our consciousness to work on our behalf in *Unveiling the Veiled*, even if we do not recognize this condition as of yet.

How can owning our truth help us? It keeps us in the Spiritual Know, giving us room to heal, restore, or regraft ourselves, increasing our instincts, the Fruits of the Spirit, and our Christlike Character.

On the other hand, lies symbolically put us into a Spiritual Coma, causing us to become clueless or reckless about what is going on from within, affecting our reality. As a result of this state of unconsciousness, unfortunately, it leaves us unbalanced, broken, and lethargic in the Realm of the Spirit, nullifying our instincts. The moment this happens, we tend to get God, ourselves, and others all wrong. Or, we may misinterpret people, places, things, and situations based on our limited perception of worldliness, false generalization, and conditional discrimination, pretending to be better than others.

We have all been conditioned to do, say, become, think, react, or behave in some manner, positively or negatively. The primary objective is to understand a few forms of conditioning to give us a better understanding of how to recognize them when encountered. Listed below are a few conditioning factors, but not limited to such:

- ☐ *Classic Conditioning* is the controlling of the likes and dislikes of a person, place, thing, or thoughts through our senses, which can be Godly or ungodly based upon the intents of the heart, environmental manipulation, or instincts.

- ☐ *Environmental Conditioning* is based on our upbringing, the people we surround ourselves with, or the behaviors we emulate based on our senses of what we see, hear, touch, taste, or smell.

- ☐ *High Mental Conditioning* judges people, places, and things, putting them into certain levels, groups, or categories based on our biases or worldliness. Unfortunately, this is where we find ourselves looking down on a certain group of people, pretending to be more than we are by keeping up a certain image for imaginary, yet worldly brownie points.

  For example, the educated look down on the uneducated, the rich look down on the poor, the Godly look down on the ungodly, etc. As a forewarning, this type of conditioning causes us to miss out on our blessings or unjustly judge someone or something we do not understand, similar to judging a book by its cover, not knowing its contents.

- ☐ *Low Mental Conditioning* is the method used to make a person feel inferior, insecure, or doubtful. This type of conditioning is often accomplished by judging, degrading, or crushing people, places, and things that appear better, superior, smarter, prettier, or more well-kept than us. In addition, this is also linked to having a negative mindset or tainted beliefs of oneself, contributing to bouts with low self-esteem or causing one to become an outright bully.

  Now, with this form of mentality beatdown, it will stimulate brow-bashing from the inside out, causing us to become our worst enemy or nightmare. So, be careful with the negatives while being quick to replace them with positive affirmations or scriptures.

- *Relational Conditioning* is wrapped in our People Skills. How we deal with, speak, or react to people we know, as well as the ones we do not, is predicated on this form of conditioning. Good, bad, or indifferent, our relational skills are a must in order to communicate; however, our effectiveness is left up to us as individuals.

- *Reinforced Conditioning* is when we are conditioned to respond or think a certain way to seemingly protect ourselves, build or crush another, bless or curse ourselves or another, and the list goes on. The bottom line is that all the behaviors, thoughts, or reactions associated with this conditioning can be unveiled positively or negatively, Godly or ungodly, justly or unjustly, calmly or irately, peacefully or chaotically, etc.

  Now, regardless of our conditioning, if we pride ourselves on continually exhibiting the Fruits of the Spirit, we will condition ourselves to respond in a Christlike manner or self-correct the moment we begin to drift to the left.

- *Punishment Conditioning* is used to break or dominate our free will. This tactic is often used by bullies, abusers, or control freaks who seek to violate the will of another, transforming the targeted victim or candidate into a desired model or mole.

  Unbeknown to most, this form of conditioning creates a double-edged sword in the Spiritual Realm. How is this possible? First, it will cause an individual to exhibit zero emotional responses or consciousness in inflicting or taking pain. For example, these are usually the ones who exhibit little or no self-control; they will pop off quickly with no regard for anyone, including God, and they are usually dominantly aggressive.

Secondly, this conditioning can swing someone all the way to the left in a pool of emotions as well, making them feel outright helpless or hopeless after any form of failure, contributing to their feelings of worthlessness. As a forewarning, with this type of conditioning, it becomes extremely hard to get rid of Spiritually. This form of conditioning hardens the heart of man, making them resistant to responding with the Fruits of the Spirit, but not exempt from doing so. They simply must work harder to undo or regraft the *'killer instinct'* of oneself or another with a Godly one.

- [ ] *Learned Conditioning* is the ability to learn from any and everything to increase one's capacity, regardless of whether it is through formal education, word-of-mouth, life of hard knocks, or Spiritual means. They are open to learning more.

- [ ] *Plan Conditioning* is where we become conditioned to set goals, create plans, develop mind maps, or strategize.

- [ ] *Nurturing Conditioning* is where we exhibit conditional love, adoration, hope, etc., based on who we feel deserves it. We often establish this relationship as siblings to institute sisterly-brotherly or parent-child relations of nurturing. If we are deprived at a young age, it will take more work to develop in adulthood.

Due to the elements of any form of known or unknown neglect, it is not easy to give what we have never experienced. For this reason, we must take it upon ourselves to overcome the hidden traumas associated with neglect, while learning more about the experience of nurturing in order to truly give it without any strings attached.

Now, on the other hand, if we are over-nurtured, we become spoiled, thinking the world must cater to us. And when it does not happen, we have a temper tantrum. Therefore, with the Nurturing Conditioning process, we must place it under a Spiritual Umbrella to create balance in this area.

- *Spiritual Conditioning* of people, places, and things in the Realm of the Spirit, usually equated in Spiritual Levels based upon the Level of Christlike Character Traits, Spiritual Fruits, and obedience to the Spiritual Classroom of Awakening. This process helps to open our Spiritual Eyes, Ears, and Mouth to our Gifts, Calling, Creativity, and Talents.

- *Biblical Conditioning* is where we learn how to align our lives Biblically. Is this the same as Spiritual Conditioning? No, it is not. Spiritual deals with Spirit and the Awakening Process; and, Biblical deals with the Word of God and the Spiritual Classroom of Alignment. But more importantly, this is where we find the applicable scriptures to align ourselves with Christlike Character and the use of the Fruits of the Spirit as it relates to our Kingdom Purpose and *As It Pleases God.*

Our conditioning is not a death sentence, nor is it set in stone. They are all changeable or negotiable as long as we master the ability to control our emotions, especially if we do not allow our thoughts to run wild, chatting waywardly, or create ungoverned illusions.

Whether we are proactive, reactive, or retroactive, we must put in the work to become the *Spiritual Sensation* God intended. How do we go about doing so? We must become masters over our natural senses and instincts, *As It Pleases Him.* Why is this so crucial? We need them to survive the wiles of the enemy, the Vicissitudes of Life, our unmet needs, and for our Divine Creativity.

Listen, every animal, whether it is a beast of the field, birds of the air, reptiles, etc., they are born with Godly, survival, and creative instincts. But more importantly, animals instinctively know when to migrate, mate, manipulate, dominate, adapt, or annihilate. If not, they perish at the mercy of another animal who uses their God-Given abilities to become a predator to easy prey. In my opinion, this is the instinctual *'Snooze You Lose'* analogy.

Spiritually, in comparison, if we snooze on our *Spiritual Senses*, we become prey as well. If we do not use our internal *Spiritual Alarm Clock* to keep watch over our Souls 24/7, we can become sideswiped in our state of slumber. Plus, if we do not train or recalibrate our instincts to the Spiritual Realm, we will become a prime target to be sifted with or without our permission. Regardless of whether we admit it or not, it is what it is! How can I say such a thing, right? Well, we will never have to teach a child how to do wrong; they already know. Yet, we must teach them how to do right, remain positive, think good thoughts, become grateful, and create a win-win.

Well, our Spiritual Instincts are like our Inner Child, which must be developed, trained, nurtured, and polished, even if we are Holy Ghost-Filled and Fire Baptized. We all know where we are in life, and if we want to sit on our hands, wanting everyone to put in the work for us, we are sadly mistaken. God's desire for us is not to distort or miscommunicate the fact that we are truly blessed to be a blessing, and we must Spiritually Till our own ground, *As It Pleases Him*.

In order for God to open the FLOODGATES of our Creativity, we must be willing to tap into our *Spiritual Senses* to become a *Spiritual Sensation*. What does this mean? Timing is everything! The moment we begin to master our instincts, we are better able to understand or recognize the Nudges of the Spirit of when to hold, when to fold, when to walk away, or when to turn our Creativity, Gifting, or Talents up a notch.

Now, the dilemma we are facing today is that we may find ourselves doing the wrong thing at the right time or the right thing at the wrong time. Meanwhile, the primary objective for the Kingdom of Heaven is that we must become adequately synced to the Spirit's leading when operating in or out of our Creativity, Gifting, Purpose, or Talents.

If we do not become Spiritually Synchronized, we may find ourselves in a cycle of déjà vu or wasting precious time, especially when we are called to maximize it. Besides, if this is the case, we must recognize it for what it is, make the necessary adjustments, or determine the conditioning contributing to the imbalance. Listed below are a few ways to become Spiritually Synced, but not limited to such:

- ☐ We must own our truth, as well as the imbalance.
- ☐ We must get an understanding of the imbalance.
- ☐ We must repent of our contributions to the imbalance.
- ☐ We must give thanks for the imbalance while ushering in what will create balance.
- ☐ We must surrender our will to the leading of the Holy Spirit.
- ☐ We must be willing to create a mind map with Divine Solutions while creating a tag team relationship from the inside out.
- ☐ We must be open to learning regardless of how difficult it may seem.
- ☐ We must cast down negative thoughts, emotions, and words by replacing them with positive, productive, and fruitful affirmations, scriptures, or truths.
- ☐ We must be willing to leave no stone unturned. Our blessings will never appear as a blessing at first; therefore, we must dig DEEP!
- ☐ We must be willing to remove our Spiritual Blinders, open our Spiritual Ears, and set a guard over our Spiritual Tongue.
- ☐ We must be willing to create a win-win out of everything and with anyone.
- ☐ We must be willing to activate the Law of Reciprocity, sharing our Creativity, Gifting, or Talents with others, *As It Pleases God.*

Can we exhibit our Creativity, Gifts, or Talents outside of God? Absolutely! However, we will not be able to use them at their full capacity without the Holy Trinity (The Father, Son, and Holy Spirit). Why can we not have it all without the Holy Trinity? First and foremost, we are Spiritual Beings; thus, we must operate in Spirit and Truth. Really? Yes, really. According to John 4:24: *"God is Spirit, and those who worship Him must worship in spirit and truth."* What does this mean? We must stop lying to God, ourselves, and others while doing things *As It Pleases Him* and not what pleases us. The bottom line is that we need our relationship with God, regardless of our justification and rationalization of our independence in our Divine Creativity, Gifting, or Talents.

Secondly, we are here for a reason outside of ourselves; however, every reason is different from person to person based upon their Divine Mission or Predestined Blueprint. Here is what 2 Corinthians 3:3 says about this: *"You are the letter from Christ, the result of our ministry, written not with ink but with the Spirit of the living God, not on the tablets of stone, but on human hearts."*

If there is any form of neglect toward our Creator, we limit ourselves by our sinful or selfish nature. If our Spirit is not AWAKENED, we will sleep on certain things by Divine Default, especially when we are required to become Spiritually Astute.

Just so we are clear, God will give us a taste of our full potential as a Spiritual Teaser. Yet, without Him, it will hang in the balance with an inner longing until we get it right. What do we need to get right? We need to get the proper Spiritual Protocol, Fruits of the Spirit, Christlike Character, or Divine Obedience right, *As It Pleases God*. For example, *"As long as Moses held up his hand, he prevailed; and when he let his hand down, Amalek prevailed."* Exodus 17:11. When we add God into the equation using our *Spiritual Senses*, we win regardless of how it appears to the natural eye.

What creates a great divide between childhood and adulthood? It is the growth process, right? The same growth process applies to our Spirituality as well, but the only difference is that we need the Holy Spirit to help us in the things of the Spirit. Is this Biblical? Absolutely. *"As for you, my son Solomon, know the God of your father, and serve Him with a loyal heart and with a willing mind; for the LORD searches all hearts and understands all the intent of the thoughts. If you seek Him, He will be found by you; but if you forsake Him, He will cast you off forever. Consider now, for the LORD has chosen you to build a house for the sanctuary; be strong, and do it."* 1 Chronicles 28:9-10.

When our heart (the Soul) is saying one thing, and our Mind is saying another, we cannot allow our Mind to run wild. If our Mind is left unguarded, consumed with negativity, lies, and debauchery, it creates open gain for the enemy, causing our soulish emotions to thwart our sense of good judgment, leaving an open door for a Spiritual Attack. So, we must close the door on the enemy by dividing the two, reeling them into what is positive, productive, fruitful, factual, and Biblical. How do we go about doing so? By behaving Christlike with the Fruits of the Spirit, thinking positively, and using Biblical Affirmations when the spark of negativity is presented to sift our Mind, Body, Soul, or Spirit.

By canceling negatives and replacing them with positivity while understanding Biblical Connotations, it becomes easier to diagnose the root cause of our issues or triggers. What makes this so important? It gives us fighting power. How is this applicable in light of what we are discussing? When our Soul is weak, our Mind is strong enough to fight on its behalf. Or, if our Mind is weak or distracted, our Soul is strong enough to fight for our sanity. Spiritually, this is one of the GREATEST DIVIDES that we miss out on in the Realm of the Spirit. Moreover, the Mind and Soul are designed to work together in UNISON to protect each other.

Yet, if we combine the Mind and Soul into one, the moment we are negatively sifted, it is much harder to break on our own or reverse the effects. As a result, we will run, shut down, lay blame, or lean on someone who is Spiritually Stronger than we are. Where is the Holy Spirit in all of this? The Holy Spirit will never override our free will. If we willfully allow our Mind and Soul to wallow in whatever contradicts the Will of God without repentance, He is limited in what He can do for us and through us.

Who limits the Holy Spirit? We do. However, all is not lost; we still have an opportunity to work on ourselves, bringing all things under the subjection of the Holy Spirit. Just keep in mind that it takes work to get to the Spiritual Level of invoking the Holy Spirit at the drop of a dime, shaking us loose from whatever or whomever, but it is doable with practice, *As It Pleases God.*

Whether we are dealing with man-made or self-made projections over our lives, we must find a way to project Love, Joy, Peace, Patience, Kindness, Goodness, Faithfulness, Gentleness, and Self-Control. Why must we project all of this? It helps us to consciously become kind and loving, *As It Pleases God.* Plus, it allows us to share the Fruits of the Spirit with no strings attached, breaking selfishness to the core. Once we pride ourselves on doing, saying, and projecting the right things, the wrong things will begin to diminish.

Darkness cannot contend with light unless there is an opening for it. So, we must master our ability to shut the door on casting doom and gloom over ourselves and others. What is the purpose of closing the door? If we leave it open, whatever we are judging, turning up our noses at, or criticizing will find its way back to our house, especially if it is not already there, creating a mirror effect. What does this mean? The reflective projections we give out will come back to us, or they are already covered up within us, positively or negatively.

So, my suggestion would be to stay on the positive side of the spectrum without judging or looking down on others. We do not know the real truth or reasoning of another man's story. We only know our own, and if we stray or teeter on the dark side, omitting our truth while finding fault in others to coax our insecurities, we may not like the results.

What are the results of darkness? The dark side will create Spiritual Planks of Blindness, Deafness, and Muteness, bringing forth dullness, deceit, assumptions, disobedience, stiff necks, and misrepresentation instead of becoming a Spiritual Lantern, bringing LIGHT into the world, *As It Pleases God.*

Chapter 12

UNVEILING THE VEILED

According to the Heavenly of Heavens, when *Unveiling The Veiled*, the lack of accountability in the Spiritual Realm is a recipe for disaster in Earthen Vessels. If we know nothing about the Spiritual Realm, it is plausible that we may remain VEILED, even if we think we have it going on or we are the hottest things since sliced bread. Nonetheless, in the Eye of God, SPIRIT is first, and all else is secondary, especially when we seek to please ourselves and pad our pockets with God nowhere in our equational efforts.

In this *Unveiling Process*, we must become truthful while correcting what lies beneath, dealing with our thoughts, emotions, fears, ungratefulness, and shame to prevent the yearning voids from taking over. Unfortunately, with zero accountability, *As It Pleases God*, it becomes easy to sell out to the highest bidder, similar to how Judas sold out Jesus with a kiss.

What does accountability have to do with Judas or us for the most part? In the Eye of God, we must learn how to query ourselves and others to establish accountability, even if it is good, bad, indifferent, or puts a bad taste in our mouths. There is always a lesson attached to whatever with whomever. *"If we have built ourselves an altar to turn from following the LORD, or if to offer on it burnt offerings or grain offerings, or if to offer peace offerings on it, let the LORD Himself require an account."* Joshua 22:23.

For the record, if we do not call an issue out for what it is, we cannot establish accountability for ourselves or others. However, we can definitely determine the contents of the hearts of those who refuse to account. Really? Yes, really! Here is the one up, *As It Pleases God*: "*Why do the wicked renounce God? He has said in his heart, 'You will not require an account.'*" Psalm 10:13.

Did Jesus make Judas give an account of his behavior? Absolutely. He did without pointing the finger, but as a question to avoid publicly outing him. Here is what I mean: "*And while He was still speaking, behold, a multitude; and he who was called Judas, one of the twelve, went before them and drew near to Jesus to kiss Him. But Jesus said to him, Judas, are you betraying the Son of Man with a kiss?*" Luke 22:47-48.

All in all, we have the Spiritual Right, *As It Pleases God*, to hold the Spirit of Deception, Betrayal, or Lies accountable. However, to do so, we must be accountable as well. If not, it leaves room for a laughable moment, lack of discernment, unrepentance, and unforgiveness. It is like calling the kettle black when we are a kettle ourselves. Plus, if we do not master asking the right fact-finding questions and using the Fruits of the Spirit, *As It Pleases God*, it becomes challenging to rattle the conscience of those with the intent to unjustifiably throw us under the bus with a kiss, smile, wink, or foul tutelage.

For example, if Jesus treated Judas like a junkyard dog, He could not rattle Judas' conscience. However, Jesus treated Judas like royalty with goodness, kindness, mercy, and love; therefore, when He asked Judas a question, his conscience did what it needed to do. What did his conscience do? CONVICT HIM!

Now, the question is, 'Can God use a sellout?' Absolutely! God uses them all the time because they become the most faithful, usable, and repenting. God likes to make an example out of us, letting us know WHO IS IN CHARGE, and He has the last say, similar to the experience with Paul on the road to Damascus.

In this life-changing event, Paul, formerly called Saul, blatantly persecuted the followers of Jesus. But the greatest miracle of all was that he wrote almost half of the New Testament, making a believer out of those who behaved similarly before his Divine Encounter.

Listen, God will use the least likely and make them likely; therefore, we should never judge a book by its cover. God will always hide Greatness, Wisdom, and Blessings in a problem, setback, disability, biases, or what we would reject. What is His reasoning for this? To provoke us, weed us out, crush us, or push us to the limit. Is this a bit much? Actually, it is good for us because the oil cannot flow without being crushed. Grapes cannot become wine without being crushed. We cannot enjoy juice without crushing the fruit, right?

To truly reap the benefits from the Fruits of the Spirit, we may experience a little crushing and disappointment in the beginning. However, once we become an EXPERT in using them, no one or nothing can hold back our Spiritual Blessings, Blueprint, or Birthright besides us. They give us the ammunition to usher in the Holy Spirit to train or cover us in the weak areas to produce Christlike Character. But if we do not know this and walk around acting foolish, resistant, unteachable, or arrogant, we may have to learn the hard way.

What is the hard way? We will experience Spiritual Blindness, Deafness, or Muteness, causing a Spiritual beat down (a void) from the inside out. In my opinion, there is nothing more humbling than God chastening us from within. Personally, I have been in this place, and I do not wish this upon my worst enemy. Therefore, if one follows my lead, this information will help self-correct the correctable while outsourcing the rest to the Holy Spirit. In addition, it will also help us take possession of our Spiritual Veil, *As It Pleases* God. Here is the deal: A Spiritual Veil is used in two ways:

- ☐ We have a Veil of Blindness, Deafness, or Muteness in the Spiritual Realm, a Divinely Designed void within the human psyche.

- ☐ We have a Veil of Protection covering those who have been Spiritually Marked for a specific Mission, similar to how we protect ourselves from viruses.

Although both Spiritual Veils are essential to the Kingdom, for the sake of this chapter, we are dealing with Spiritual Blindness, Deafness, or Muteness, removing the veil of worldliness. Is the Spiritual Veil Biblical? Yes, it is. According to 2 Corinthians 3:14-16, here is what we must know: *"But their minds were blinded. For until this day the same veil remains unlifted in the reading of the Old Testament, because the veil is taken away in Christ. But even to this day, when Moses is read, a veil lies on their heart. Nevertheless when one turns to the Lord, the veil is taken away."*

Why do we need to be Spiritually Unveiled? Most often, amid living life, we do not realize we are Spiritually Veiled until we require Spiritual Insight, Divine Restoration, or when we have to depend upon the Spiritual Strength of another to fill a need. But more importantly, if we have a desire to become liberated Mentally, Physically, Emotionally, and Spiritually, the worldly veil must go. Is this Biblical? I would have it no other way! *"Now the Lord is the Spirit; and where the Spirit of the Lord is, there is liberty. But we all, with unveiled face, beholding as in a mirror the glory of the Lord, are being transformed into the same image from glory to glory, just as by the Spirit of the Lord."* 2 Corinthians 3:17-18.

In *Unveiling the Veiled* or becoming a *Mirror of Christ*, we must transform our way of thinking, behaving, and communicating from worldly to Godly. If we think about it for a minute, most of our precious time is used to solve people's problems, whether at home, on the job, at church, or wherever, with little or no time to work on ourselves. So, what do we do? We unintentionally omit our inner self, and then blame or justify our reasons for self-neglect.

As a result of our oversight, neglect, or veiled understanding, we overcompensate by becoming selfish, materialistic, arrogant, rude, covetous, jealous, envious, hateful, and condescending without realizing the reasons why. But, there is hope for all, and if we peel back the layers blinding us, we will see the resolve we are in need of, or we may receive the answers to our dilemma that resides within.

According to the Heavenly of Heavens, we are not here to fix people. It is God's job to fix the hole in us and them! Here is what

Matthew 7:5 advises: *"First remove the plank from your own eye, and then you will see clearly to remove the speck from your brother's eye."*

Once we are done working on ourselves from the inside out, we then become the Lamp of Light, illuminating the lives of others by setting an example, mentoring, teaching, building, and sharing with the Fruits of the Spirit in hand while exhibiting Christlike Character.

As we go a little deeper regarding the Pit, we must also realize it is connected to our Spiritual Seals as well. Blasphemy, right? Wrong again, let us take it to scripture, *"Then the fifth angel sounded: And I saw a star fallen from heaven to the earth. To him was given the key to the bottomless pit. And he opened the bottomless pit, and smoke arose out of the pit like the smoke of a great furnace. So the sun and the air were darkened because of the smoke of the pit. Then out of the smoke locusts came upon the earth. And to them was given power, as the scorpions of the earth have power. They were commanded not to harm the grass of the earth, or any green thing, or any tree, but only those men who do not have the seal of God on their foreheads. And they were not given authority to kill them, but to torment them for five months. Their torment was like the torment of a scorpion when it strikes a man. In those days men will seek death and will not find it; they will desire to die, and death will flee from them."* Revelation 9:1-6. What does this mean? If we do not have the Spiritual Seal, inner trauma, stress, oppression, and cluelessness will come upon us from the inside out.

Listen, most are looking for a physical Pit because we are visual by nature. Yet, Spiritually Speaking, the Pit is buried within our soul as a colorless, odorless, and tasteless krypton, choking the life out of us Mentally, Physically, Emotionally, and Spiritually. More importantly, if we do not Spiritually Awaken our Spirit to engage in a *Spirit to Spirit* communion or ordination process, *As It Pleases God*; unfortunately, inner torment will come upon us, spreading outwardly with the boiling over fumes from within and getting on those around us.

Yet, due to our Spiritual Blindness, Deafness, and Muteness, we are unable to protect ourselves from the inside out. We do not have the Spiritual Marking or Seal granting us Spiritual Immunity, a Pass Over, or Divine Covering.

Do we not have the free will to accept or reject the seals? Of course, God will not violate our free will; however, we do not want to get caught up in unrepentant sin. Why should we avoid getting caught up in such a manner as Believers? By getting willfully caught up, we can bring about plagues and curses into our lives, as well as into our Bloodlines. Is this Biblical? Absolutely! *"But the rest of mankind, who were not killed by these plagues, did not repent of the works of their hands, that they should not worship demons, and idols of gold, silver, brass, stone, and wood, which can neither see nor hear nor walk. And they did not repent of their murders or their sorceries or their sexual immorality or their thefts."* Revelation 9:20-21. I could not make this up if I tried, so take heed to *The Great Reveal*.

We often think God is a little harsh in how He deals with His Divine Creation, but if the truth is told, He has MERCIFULLY designed our lives to heal themselves. Yet, we become so busy living the lives of another that we ignore what life is saying, nor do we take heed to the leading of the Lord, *As it Pleases Him*.

Meanwhile, due to this Spiritual Omission and to please ourselves, we get caught up in bickering, fussing, fighting, and complaining about people, places, and things that have nothing to do with our story or Divine Blueprint. Then again, we become consumed with who is right or wrong, better or worse, stronger or weaker, blessed or cursed, holy or unholy, or this and that. When we get caught up in such a manner, we will find that jealousy, envy, coveting, competitiveness, hatefulness, rudeness, pride, and unkindness will cause us to become secretly or openly bitter and unforgiving. In the Eye of God, behaving in such a manner will cause the psyche to implode from the inside out and explode from the outside in.

According to the Heavenly of Heavens, if we create a win-win with our lives, we can overcome with the Power of our Testimony. Here is another one up for the Kingdom: *"So I went to the angel and said to him, 'Give me the little book.' And he said to me, 'Take and eat it; and it will make your stomach bitter, but it will be as sweet as honey in your mouth.'* Then

I took the little book out of the angel's hand and ate it, and it was as sweet as honey in my mouth. But when I had eaten it, my stomach became bitter. And he said to me, You must prophesy again about many peoples, nations, tongues, and kings." Revelation 10:9-11.

We are the book that keeps on giving. Once we are Spiritually Unveiled, we cannot stop at one miracle, especially when we are full of miracles. Really? Yes, really! What do we need to do to create an abundance of miracles? We need to open our mouths positively, allowing God to ABIDE, *As It Pleases Him*. But, do not take my word for it; let us take it to scripture, *"I am the LORD your God, Who brought you out of the land of Egypt; Open your mouth wide, and I will fill it."* Psalm 81:10. *"If you abide in Me, and My words abide in you, you will ask what you desire, and it shall be done for you."* John 15:7.

Since the Spiritual Veil is now broken, *As It Pleases God*, grow GREAT, and many Blessings to all.

Dr. Y. Bur

www.ingramcontent.com/pod-product-compliance
Lightning Source LLC
Chambersburg PA
CBHW071428160426
43195CB00013B/1840